THREE VIS
TO
EARLY PLYMOUTH

LETTERS ABOUT THE PILGRIM SETTLEMENT IN NEW ENGLAND
DURING ITS FIRST SEVEN YEARS

BY JOHN PORY, EMMANUEL ALTHAM
AND ISAACK DE RASIERES

foreword by
JAMES W. BAKER

introduction by
SAMUEL ELIOT MORISON

edited by
SYDNEY V. JAMES, JR.

APPLEWOOD BOOKS
BEDFORD, MASSACHUSETTS

Three Visitors to Early Plymouth was first published by the Plimoth Plantation, Inc., in 1963.

"Foreword to the Second Printing" Copyright © 1997 by James W. Baker.

Thank you for purchasing an Applewood Book.
Applewood reprints America's lively classics—books from the past that are of interest to modern readers. For a free catalog of our current publications, write to: Applewood Books, P.O. Box 365, Bedford, MA 01730.

ISBN 1-55709-463-2

Printed in the United States of America

Library of Congress Catalog Card Number: 97-72967

Contents

FOREWORD TO THE SECOND PRINTING

H ISTORIANS of Plymouth Colony have been particularly fortunate in that large numbers of primary source
documents have survived. The official records of the
colony from the 1630s until 1692, which include the acts of the
General Court, laws, deeds, probate inventories and others, are
as complete or more so than those of any other colony. The
anonymous *Mourt's Relation*, Edward Winslow's *Good Newes from
New England*, and William Bradford's *Of Plymouth Plantation* provide us with an unusually thorough account of the colony's
early years.

Despite the wealth of information that is available, there are
always more questions than answers. We think wistfully how
wonderful it would be if only a few more facts had been preserved, or if the early writers had been prescient enough to
record the details of everyday life we find so interesting but they
took for granted. There is always the hope that a new treasure
trove of original papers might be discovered in some forgotten
repository or private collection, as Governor Bradford's manuscript was—or the letters reproduced in *Three Visitors to Early
Plymouth* were.

These letters not only corroborate information that we find
in the other sources, but also preserve intimate details about
New Plymouth that would otherwise have been forgotten to history. John Pory, for example, provides us with the specific
dimensions (2,700 feet in compass) of the palisade erected
around the town in 1622, and notes that it was stronger than
any he had seen in Virginia. Emmanual Altham adds that the
pales were about eight feet high. Altham also records that the

Pilgrims' Wampanoag neighbor and advisor, Hobbamock, had more than one wife and a family of "above ten persons," which is invaluable for the interpretation of the Hobbamock Homesite exhibit at Plimoth Plantation.

If only the account of the "First Thanksgiving" survived, we might think that the Native participation in the 1621 Plymouth event was a unique occurrence, but Altham informs us that not only did Massasoit attend Governor Bradford's wedding in 1623 with one of his five wives and 60 men, but also presented the Governor with "three or four deer and a turkey."

The most interesting account, however, is that of the Dutch *Opper Koopman*, Isaack de Rasieres. This letter has not only provided the insipiration for the "Pilgrims Progress" march that has been re-enacted in downtown Plymouth each year since 1921, but by its excellent description of the Pilgrim settlement in the year 1627, also helped determine the scope of Plimoth Plantation's Pilgrim Village re-creation.

It is unlikely that there will be more great Plymouth Colony discoveries. The public's long fascination with the Pilgrims and anything associated with them insured that such records as have survived were long since recognized and rescued from oblivion. However, it is always possible that another unknown observer's account of early Plymouth will be found. We can only hope that the future might bring a *Four Visitors to Early Plymouth*!

JAMES W. BAKER
Chief Historian
Plimoth Plantation
April 1997

Introduction

WE ALL KNOW what the Pilgrim Fathers wrote about themselves and their settlements on the (not so) "stern and rockbound coast"; but how many people know that they were visited thrice, between 1622 and 1627, by outsiders who left on record candid accounts of what they saw? That is the reason for this book. These three accounts — one by a gentleman from Virginia, one by an Englishman straight from England, and the other by a Dutchman from New Amsterdam — are brought together between two covers, so that we can see how the Pilgrims and New Plymouth appeared to visitors who shared neither their particular beliefs nor their intention to live in New England.

John Pory's, the Virginian account, was discovered early in this century and published in a small limited edition, long since out of print. De Rasieres' Dutch account is best known; it was discovered in mid-nineteenth century, was promptly translated, and has several times been printed. Three of the Altham letters have never before been printed. The manuscripts were purchased by the late Dr. Otto Fisher, who kindly permitted us to publish this *editio princeps*. The fourth Altham letter, printed some years ago, has been included, as it rounds out the story.

Pory's account is valuable for the vivid description of the bounties of nature at Plymouth and along the coast of Maine. We are sorry he did not have time to investigate the Indians' tall tale of mammoth Massachusetts oysters. He confirms Edward Winslow's story about Governor Bradford's exchange of diplomatic messages (snakeskin and bullets) with Canonicus, somewhat suggesting what now goes on between Washington and

Moscow. Bradford refers pleasantly to Pory's visit in his *Of Plymouth Plantation* chapter xiii, and notes that he borrowed the Governor's copy of Henry Ainsworth's *Annotations upon the Fourth Book of Moses* for shipboard reading on his passage to England.

The Altham letters provide the first new information about the Plymouth Colony to appear in fifty years. Captain Emmanuel Altham of the pinnace *Little James*, which arrived at Plymouth in 1623, gives us a fresh description of the settlement, its meager resources in livestock, and its abundant store of fish and timber. An important item for Pilgrim lore is the description of Bradford's marriage feast, which the Governor was too modest to include in his History. Altham gives a vivid characterization of Massasoit, the guest of honor, and notes the delicacy of that chieftain in bringing only one of his five wives to the party. And he corroborates Winslow's story of Miles Standish's expedition against Wessagusset.

Altham, as one of the English Adventurers who financed Plymouth Colony, adds appreciably to our knowledge of how that business was done. He thoroughly disapproves of the faction among the Adventurers that was responsible for inflicting the Rev. John Lyford on Plymouth. Altham's present to his brother of a "great king's pipe" that "doth stink exceedingly of Indian tobacco" makes a humorous postscript to this very interesting series of letters.

De Rasieres' letters, although well known, have never before been printed in so full and accurate a translation. They open with a description of Manhattan Island only three years after the settlement of New Amsterdam, and of the shores of Long Island Sound. They describe Algonkian Indian customs such as the making of wampum, the growing of Indian corn, with recipes for corn bread and porridge, and methods of dealing with unfaithful wives and roving husbands. Once arrived at New Plymouth, De Rasieres describes the settlement with great care—the clapboarded houses, the square fort on Burial Hill, and the Sabbath church parade to beat of drum, which has become classic. Nor does he neglect the government of the colony or the customs of the neighboring Indians.

Detractors of the Pilgrim Colony will find no ammunition in these three contemporary descriptions. The Virginian, the Englishman, and the Dutchman found much to admire in the Colony and nothing to disparage. They have given us fresh reason to respect the faith and fortitude of that little band in its struggle to maintain a toe hold on the edge of the American wilderness.

SAMUEL ELIOT MORISON

February 1963

Editor's Preface

LETTERS which have survived over three hundred years, escaping the ravages of fire, water, vermin, and people who wanted to wrap fish, have a claim to our respect. All the more so if they shed light on a subject of as widespread interest as early Plymouth. As editor of the letters presented here, therefore, I had better explain what has happened to them in my hands and make it known that my intentions were honorable. In order to win as many readers for these letters as possible, I have put them into modern style in certain respects. To those written originally in English, the letters by Emmanuel Altham and John Pory, I have given modern spelling without changing the words, and punctuation to make them into sentences and paragraphs in twentieth-century fashion as much as possible. I have followed the general approach described by Samuel Eliot Morison in the preface to his edition of William Bradford's *Of Plymouth Plantation* (New York, 1952), pp. vii–ix. I have also followed his example in many details, such as spellings. However, anything Pory or Altham wrote which is acceptable to modern usage has been left alone, regardless of consistency within this book. I have standardized proper names ruthlessly, except for some which have no modern or official form, as is the case with most old Dutch place names. Since Isaack De Rasieres' Dutch has been translated directly into modern English, it has not needed the same treatment.

Footnotes have been supplied mainly to give information useful for an understanding of the letters, not exhaustive comparisons with other documents. Some notes give original spellings which others may not wish to modernize as I have done it in the text. Bibliographical information in the footnotes is supplemented by the bibliographical note at the end of the book.

The dates used in the letters are reproduced exactly. This means that they are of the Julian Calendar or Old Style, used by Englishmen until September 1752. In the biographical sketches of the letter writers, also, the old dating system has been followed. Not only was the day of the month different from the modern calendar (during the 1600's Old Style dates ran ten days behind New Style, so that December 11, o.s., was December 21, N.S.) but the beginning of the year was reckoned from March 25, although all of March was called the first month of the year. This confused even the users of the Julian Calendar, who frequently tried to prevent mistakes by giving both the outgoing and the incoming year numbers to dates in March before the 25th—for example, March 9, 1629/1630. Hoping to minimize confusion for the modern reader, I have adopted a rarer version of this practice, giving two year numbers to all dates from January 1 to March 24.

JOHN PORY

NEW ENGLAND ABOUT 1625

SCALE 0 — 50 MILES

NOTE: Later names appear in brackets

1 North River
2 Jones River
3 Billington Sea & Town Brook
4 Eel River
5 Manomet River

N

Pentagoet [Penobscot] R.

Androscoggin R.

Kennebec R.

←Pemaquid
Monhegan I.
Damerill's Cove
[Damariscove I.]

Sagadahoc R.

Piscataqua R.
Isles of Shoals

Cape Ann
Anquam [Annisquam?]
[Gloucester]

ATLANTIC OCEAN

MASSACHUSETTS

[Blackstone R.]

Wessagussett

Cohasset

1

Cape Cod Harbor [Provincetown]

2
3   Plymouth
4

Pamet [Truro]

WAMPANOAG
INDIANS

5

Nauset [Eastham]

Pocanocket

Aptuxcet

NARRAGANSETT
INDIANS

Cape Malabar
[Monomoy Point]

Buzzard's Bay

Capawack or
Martha's Vineyard

[Sakonnet R.]
[Narragansett Bay]

Fisher's [Montauk] Point

V∕R

John Pory (1572-1635)

JOHN PORY had led a full life before he visited Plymouth and New England in 1622, on his way home from a three-year term as Secretary to the Governor and Council of Virginia. Born into the family of a Norfolk gentleman, a graduate of Gonville and Caius College, Cambridge, he had been an apprentice to the great historian of English seafaring, Richard Hakluyt. After producing a successful book on Africa in 1600, he left the scholarly life, served eminent men as private correspondent on news from London, sat in Parliament from 1605 to 1611, acted as aide to various diplomats, went on missions for King James I and his Privy Council, and traveled in Ireland, France, Italy, Greece, and Turkey. By 1619, when he received his Virginia appointment, he had many friends, a restless foot, large girth, and fondness for wine.

The New World was a strange one for Pory, but always optimistic, he turned his back on conviviality and news of the capital to accept water and good books with enthusiasm. He also made a name for himself as an explorer on a small scale and earned lasting fame as the very able speaker of the first colonial assembly, called in 1619.

Even before leaving England for America, Pory embroiled himself in the party strife which led to the downfall of the Virginia Company in 1624. Appointed by the "ins," at the request of his cousin, Gov. Yeardley, Pory ultimately sided with the group led by the Earl of Warwick, the "outs" from 1619 to 1624. He earned an appointment to the panel of Commissioners to inspect affairs in Virginia for the Privy Council in 1624, and on his return, received a place on the board chosen to establish

3

royal government in the colony. He spent several years at his old occupation of London correspondent before he made his home in Lincolnshire, where he died in 1635.

John Pory stopped at New England on his way back to England partly on Company business. Ships had often gone north from Virginia to fish, before the king granted monopoly rights over fishing to the Council for New England, created in 1620. The Virginia Company thought its interests damaged, continued to sell licenses to fish in the disputed area, and futilely protested the monopoly in the Privy Council. Pory was to get the Company firsthand information about the fishing business in New England, see what the Council for New England was actually doing, and assess the prospects of the Plymouth settlement. The extracts from his letters which follow were probably written as reports.

The originals of Pory's letters are gone, as far as anyone knows. What exists is a copy, probably made by Richard Norwood, surveyor of the "Summer Isles" (Bermudas). The manuscript is unsigned, undated and consists of extracts from two letters by John Pory and a description of Bermuda by Norwood. It is in the John Carter Brown Library, Providence, Rhode Island. The whole text, edited, annotated, and introduced by Champlin Burrage, was printed under the title, *John Pory's Lost Description of Plymouth in the Earliest Days of the Pilgrim Fathers* (1918). This edition, plus photostats of the manuscript, were used in the preparation of the text printed here.

John Pory to the Earl of Southampton[1]

January 13, 1622/1623, and later.

By whom this New Plymouth (situated, according to Captain Jones[2] his computation, in 41 degrees and 48 minutes) is now presently inhabited, your Lordship and the honorable Company do know better than myself. For whom how favourably God's providence in thought and in deed, quite besides any plot or design of theirs, hath wrought, especially in the beginning of their enterprise, is worthy to be observed. For when, as your Lordship knows, their voyage was intended for Virginia, being by letters from Sir Edwin Sandys and Mr. Deputy Ferrar recommended to Sir Yeardley[3] (then Governor) that he should give them the best advice he could for trading in Hudson's River, whether it were by contrariety of wind or by the backwardness of their master or pilot[4] to make (as they thought it) too long a journey, they fell short both of the one and the other, arriving first at that stately harbour called Cape Cod,[5] called by Indians

1. Henry Wriothesley, Earl of Southampton, Treasurer (chief executive) of the Virginia Company of London, 1620–24.
2. Thomas Jones, Captain of the *Discovery*, the ship in the service of the Virginia Company on which Pory was traveling. (Not to be confused with Christopher Jones, master of the *Mayflower* in 1620.)
3. Sandys was Treasurer of the Virginia Company, 1619–20, a notable Puritan and opponent of royal absolutism, influential in granting a patent to the Pilgrims and their backers permitting them to establish a "particular plantation" in Virginia, which then extended as far north as 41°, thus including the mouth of the Hudson River. John Ferrar was Deputy to the Treasurer in 1620. Sir George Yeardley, knighted and sent out as Governor to Virginia in 1619, was the candidate of Sandys's party.
4. Christopher Jones or John Clarke, a pilot experienced in the northern route to Virginia (on which a ship sighted land at or near Cape Cod and proceeded down the coast to Chesapeake Bay).
5. Provincetown, Mass.

"Pamet"; from whence in shallop the pilot, a more forward undertaker than performer, promised to bring them to be seated in a pleasant and fertile place called Anquam,[6] situate within Cape Ann,[7] about forty leagues from Plymouth. After some dangerous and almost incurable errors and mistakings, he stumbled by accident upon the harbour of Plymouth; where, after the planters had failed of their intention, and the pilot of his, it pleased Almighty God (who had better provided for them than their own hearts could imagine) to plant them on the seat of an old town which divers [years] before had been abandoned of the Indians. So they both quietly and justly sate down without either dispossessing any of the natives, or being resisted by them, and without shedding so much as one drop of blood. Which felicity of theirs is confirmed unto them even by the voices of the savages themselves, who generally do acknowledge not only the seat, but the whole seigniory[8] thereto belonging, to be, and do themselves disclaim all title from it; so that the right of those planters to it is altogether unquestionable—a favor which, since the first discovery of America, God hath not vouchsafed, so far as ever I could learn, upon any Christian nation within that continent. Yet can it not be denied but that these of the Summer Islands[9] are blessed with the same privilege according to the saying of St. Paul, "If the firstfruits be holy, the lump is also holy."[10]

But to leave this privilege to them whom it concerns, and to describe to your Lordship the excellency of the place. First, the

6. Gloucester or Annisquam, Mass.

7. "Anna" in the manuscript.

8. Englishmen tended to translate Indian customs into feudal law. Plymouth and the territory around it had been the home of a tribal group of which Squanto was the only survivor. Neighboring Indians traditionally had no rights there. The Pilgrims interpreted the claims of Massasoit, the Wampanoag chief, as feudal overlordship over southeastern Massachusetts, so the vacant parts of it which they took up logically had to be a feudal domain of some kind.

9. Bermudas.

10. Romans 11:16.

harbour is not only pleasant for air and prospect, but most sure for shipping, both small and great, being land-locked on all sides. The town is seated on the ascent of a hill, which besides the pleasure of variable objects entertaining the unsatisfied eye, such is the wholesomeness of the place (as the Governor[11] told me) that for the space of one whole year of the two wherein they had been there, died not one man, woman or child.

This healthfulness is accompanied with much plenty both of fish and fowl every day in the year, as I know no place in the world that can match it. In March the eels come forth out of places where they lie bedded all winter, into the fresh streams, and there into the sea, and in their passages are taken in pots. In September they run out of the sea into the fresh streams, to bed themselves in the ground all winter, and are taken again in pots as they return homewards. In winter the inhabitants dig them up, being bedded in gravel not above two or three foot deep, and all the rest of the year they may take them in pots in the salt water of the bay. They are passing sweet, fat and wholesome, having no taste at all of the mud, and are as great as ever I saw any.

In April and May come up another kind of fish which they call herring or old wives[12] in infinite schools, into a small river[13] running under the town, and so into a great pond or lake of a mile broad, where they cast their spawn, the water of the said river being in many places not above half a foot deep. Yea, when a heap of stones is reared up against them a foot high above the water, they leap and tumble over, and will not be beaten back with cudgels. Which confirmeth not only that of Horace, "*Naturam expellas furca licet*," etc.,[14] but that also which was

11. William Bradford.
12. Alewives.
13. Town Brook.
14. The whole passage reads: "Naturam expelles furca licet, tamen usque recurret, et mala perrumpet furtim fastidia victrix." "You may drive out Nature with a pitchfork, yet she will ever hurry back, and, ere you know it, will burst through your

thought a fable of Friar Beatus Odoricus, namely, that in some
parts where he had travelled, the fish in the springtime did cast
themselves out of the sea upon the dry land.[15] The inhabitants
during the said two months take them up every day in hogsheads. And with those they eat not they manure the ground,
burying two or three in each hill of corn—and may, when they
are able, if they see cause, lade whole ships with them. At their
going up they are very fat and savory, but at their coming down,
after they have cast their spawns, they are shot, and therefore
lean and unwholesome. Into another river some two miles to the
northeast of Plymouth,[16] all the month of May the great smelts
pass up to spawn, likewise in troops innumerable, which with a
scoop or a bowl, or a piece of bark, a man may cast up upon the
bank.

About mid-May come into the harbour the main school of
bass and bluefish, which they take with seines[17]—some fishes of
a foot and a half, some of two foot, and some of three foot long—
and with hooks, those of four and five foot long. They enter also
at flowing water[18] up into the small creeks, at the mouths whereof the inhabitants, spreading their nets, have caught 500 and 700
at a time. These continue good May, June, July and August.
Now as concerning the bluefish, in delicacy it excelleth all kind
of fish that ever I tasted; I except not the salmon of the Thames
in his prime season, nor any other fish. We called it by a com-

---

foolish contempt in triumph." Horace, "Epistles, Book I, Epistle x," *Satires, Epistles
and Ars Poetica* with English translation by H. Rushton Fairclough (Loeb Classical
Library, 1932), 316, 317.

15. Odoric of Pordenone (c. 1286–1331, formally beatified in the eighteenth century) was a Franciscan friar and missionary who traveled widely in the Far East. The
story of his travels became popular in the fourteenth century, but fell from favor as it
gained a reputation for embroidery. The phenomenon to which Pory refers occurred
at a place described as "Moumoran" in the printed version with which Pory was
probably familiar, that in Hakluyt, *Principal Navigations* (1599), II, 57.

16. A stream running from the Smelt Pond to Plymouth Bay, entering it at the
mouth of the Jones River, about two miles northwest of Plymouth.

17. "Skeines" in the manuscript.

18. High tide in tidal streams.

pound name of black, white, blue, sweet, fat—the skin and scale, blue; the flesh next under the scale for an inch deep, black and as sweet as the marrow of an ox; the residue of the flesh underneath, purely white, fat, and of a taste requiring no addition of sauce. By which alluring qualities it may seem dangerously tending to a surfeit, but we found by experience that having satisfied (and in a manner glutted) ourselves therewith, it proved wholesome unto us and most easy of digestion.

In the same bay, lobsters are in season during the four months —so large, so full of meat, and so plentiful in number as no man will believe that hath not seen. For a knife of three halfpence, I bought ten lobsters that would well have dined forty labouring men. And the least boy in the ship, with an hour's labour, was able to feed the whole company with them for two days; which, if those of the ship that come home do not affirm upon their oaths, let me forever lose my credit!

Without the bay, in the ocean sea, they have all the year long in a manner goodly fishing of cod and hake, as in other parts of Canada. Within two miles southward from their plantation do begin goodly ponds and lakes of fresh water, continuing well nigh twenty miles into the land, some with islands in them, the water being as clear as crystal, yielding great variety of fish.

Mussels and clams[19] they have all the year long; which, being the meanest of God's blessings here, and such as these people fat their hogs with at a low water, if ours upon any extremity did enjoy in the South Colony,[20] they would never complain of famine or want, although they wanted bread. (Not but that, by God's blessing, the South Colony using their industry may in few years attain to that plenty, pleasure and strength as that they shall not need much to envy or fear the proudest nations in Europe.) Oysters there are none, but at Massachusetts, some 20 miles to the north of this place, there are such huge ones, by savages' report, as I am loth to report. For ordinary ones, of

---

19. "Muskles and slammes" in the manuscript.   20. Virginia.

which there be many, they make to be as broad as a bushel, but one among the rest they compared to the great cabin of the *Discovery*, and being sober and well-advised persons, grew very angry when they were laughed at or not believed! I would have had Captain Jones to have tried out the truth of this report. And what was the reason? If, said I, the oysters be so great and have any pearls in them, then must the pearls be answerable in greatness to the oysters, and proving round and orient also, would far exceed all other jewels in the world! Yea, what strange and precious things might be found in so rare a creature! But Captain Jones his employing his pinnace in discovery, his graving of the ship, his haste away about other occasions and business, would not permit him to do that which often since he wished he could have done.

From the beginning of September till the end of March, their bay in a manner is covered with all sorts of water fowl, in such sort of swarms and multitudes as is rather admirable than credible. The reasons of their continual plenty for those seven months in the year may be their continual tranquility of the place, being guarded on all sides from the fury of the storms; as also the abundance of food they find at low water, the bottom of the bay then appearing as a green meadow; and lastly, the number of freshets running into the bay, where after their powdered salads, their brackish shellfish and other cates,[21] they may refresh and quench their thirst. And therefore, this bay is such a pond for fowl as in any man's knowledge of our nation that hath seen it, all America hath not the like.

(Thus far I proceeded and dated my letter at Angra,[22] Jan. 13, 1622[/1623].)

Touching their fruit, I will not speak of their meaner sort, as of rasps,[23] cherries, gooseberries, strawberries, delicate plums

21. Delicacies.
22. Chief town on Terceira, one of the Azore Islands, where Pory was detained a prisoner on his way to England.
23. Raspberries.

and others. But they have commonly through the country five
several sorts of grapes, some whereof I tasted, being fairer and
larger than any I ever saw in the South Colony, but of a muscatel
taste,[24] which being transplanted, would prosper better in the
south. But wine vines may compare with Martha's Vineyard,
which I dare say will fall to the south of 40 degrees,[25] and will be
an earthly paradise to him that can be master of it. Sassafras
wanteth not all over this main. In this land, as in other parts of
this main, they have plenty of deer and of turkeys as large and
as fat as in any other place.

So much of the wholesomeness and plenty of the country.
Now as concerning the quality of the people, how happy were it
for our people in the Southern Colony, if they were as free from
wickedness and vice as these are in this place! And their industry as well appeareth by their building, as by a substantial palisado about their [town] of 2700 foot in compass, stronger than
I have seen any in Virginia, and lastly by a blockhouse which
they have erected in the highest place of the town to mount their
ordnance upon, from whence they may command all the harbour.

As touching their correspondence with the Indians, they are
friends with all their neighbours—as namely with those of Cohasset[26] and Massachusetts to the north, with the great king of
Pocanocket[27] to the southwest, with those of Pamet, Nauset,
Capawack[28] and others to the east and south. And notwithstanding that those of the isle Capawack are mortal enemies to all
other English, ever since Hunt most wickedly stole away their
people to sell them for slaves,[29] yet are they in good terms with

24. The "musky" flavor common to the muscat grape varieties. "Muskadell" in
the manuscript.

25. Pory was wrong; it is north of 41°.

26. "Conahassit," an old form, in the manuscript.

27. Massasoit, chief of the Wampanoag or Pocanocket Indians, who lived in the
territory around present-day Bristol, R. I., which was then called Pocanocket.

28. Pamet is present-day Truro, Nauset is the area from Eastham to the Denises,
both on Cape Cod. Capawack is the island, Martha's Vineyard.

29. Capt. Thomas Hunt took two dozen Indians captive in 1614, some at Ply-

them of Plymouth, because as they never did wrong to any Indians, so will they put up no injury at their hands. And though they gave them kind entertainment, yet stand they day and night precisely upon their guard. True it is that Narragansett,[30] situate to the west of Pocanocket, being set on either by the French or Flemings,[31] sent them a snake's skin full of arrows in token of hostility and defiance. In answer whereof, having filled the same with shot and powder, they sent it back again with this message: that whensoever[32] he should be welcome, and should find them ready to entertain him. The shot and powder he liked not, nor would meddle with it, but caused it to be cast into the river.

One thing which made them to be much respected was the revenge which they attempted in the night upon Corbitant,[33] the chief man about the great king, because they were (though falsely) informed that he had slain Tisquanto, Sir Ferdinando Gorges his Indian,[34] who lived as their servant under their protection, interpreting the injury done to him as done to themselves. Besides, when Tisquanto was earnestly required to be

mouth, some on Cape Cod, and sold several as slaves at Málaga. While Hunt's deeds were not excusable, they were merely the worst of several such incidents. Capt. John Smith pointed out that Hunt could not be responsible for the special hostility of the Capawack Indians toward the English. Rather, their ill will may be traced to the kidnaping of Epenow and Coneconam by Capt. Harlow, in 1614 or earlier; the series of degrading experiences which Epenow underwent at the hands of English captors; his influence on his countrymen after his return to Capawack; and the somewhat mysterious friction between him and Capt. Dermer in 1620, in which the latter was mortally wounded. The Capawack Indians probably feared reprisal for this and related incidents. Capt. John Smith, *Generall Historie of Virginia, New England, and the Summer Isles* (1632), 204–205; Samuel Purchas, *Hakluytus Posthumus or Purchas His Pilgrimes* (1625), IV, 1778, 1828, 1841, 1849; James P. Baxter, *Sir Ferdinando Gorges and His Province of Maine* (Prince Society, 1890), I, 104n–106n; W. F. Gookin, *Capawack alias Martha's Vineyard* (1947), 8–17.

30. Canonicus, the Narragansett sachem.
31. Netherlanders who traded around the mouth of the Hudson River before the actual founding of New Amsterdam in 1626.
32. Whenever the king might come.
33. "Combotant" in the manuscript.
34. Squanto, the Pilgrims' friend and sole survivor of the Patuxet natives, had

sent home by the great king, they choose rather to hazard a falling out with him than to break their faith and promise with Tisquanto, who had been sure to have gone to the pot if they had delivered him up. Which faith and courage of theirs hath made other distracted Indians to retire themselves into their protection, of whose labour and service they have made good use, but especially of Tisquanto's.

And since I have taken occasion to speak both of amity and enmity, give me leave to note unto your Lordship the general enemy of all, both Christians and Indians in Canada, that inhabit toward the ocean, being (as they of New Plymouth relate) an Indian nation of man-eaters called Mohawks,[35] who go armed against arrows with jacks[36] made of cordage, and they themselves use clubs only.

Of the language of the natives about Plymouth and Cape Cod I have collected a small dictionary, wherein I find many words agreeing with those of the South Colony and of the eastern shore of the bay.[37] I have one great design; namely, to find out what sea that is, which the Frenchmen put down in their cards[38] to west in 40 degrees over against the bottom of the said bay, whether or no an inlet of the South Sea.[39] It must be done, by the grace of God, through the guidance of the Susquehannas,[40] a most barbarous nation and supposed to be man-eaters. Yet upon this condition I will adventure myself with them by land: if I may have a convenient bark [in which] to keep for my security three or four hostages.

---

been one of the Indians gathered by Sir Ferdinando to get information about New England. Gorges sent him back to America in 1618 or 1619 as guide to Capt. Dermer.

35. "Monhaccke" in the manuscript. In the early seventeenth century, Iroquois Indians ranged as far east as New Hampshire.

36. Hip-length coats of some protective strength.

37. Eastern shore of Chesapeake Bay, where Pory had held land.

38. Charts.

39. Pacific Ocean. The French knew about the Great Lakes.

40. Indians, quite powerful in Pory's day, living in the lower part of the river valley of the same name.

John Pory to the Governor of Virginia (Sir Francis Wyatt)

Autumn, 1622.

Whereas heretofore a vulgar error, namely that fish is not to be had here[1] at all times of the year, had generally possessed the minds of all men, experience hath now taught us the contrary: that in some two months of the cod, which never bites but in the daytime, comes altogether as good a fish called a hake, to be caught in the night. The places of fishing upon this coast are as universal as the times, for it is experimented now by one John Gibbs,[2] who this summer hath passed five or six times between this place and New Plymouth, that a man cannot cast out a hook at any ledge at sea in that distance, but he shall draw up goodly fish at pleasure—upon whose relation divers mean to fish the next year more toward the southwest. And Cape Cod itself hath not that name for naught: for it is thought that one shallop's fishing only would suffice the whole plantation of New Plymouth all the year long. To the east and north of this place is found as great plenty as to the south and west. Now whether there be any cod or no to the south of the place (as the Company[3] desire to be informed), although Mr. Vengham,[4] a man of experience in those parts, do seem to doubt. Yet a Flemish[5] pilot, who is to

1. The letter was written at the fishing grounds off northern New England, probably Monhegan.
2. In 1628 John Gibbs was master of the *Marmaduke* in the service of the New Plymouth Adventurers.
3. Virginia Company of London.
4. William Vengham. He was living and selling cured fish at Monhegan (probably by arrangement with the island's owners) in 1624, and perhaps when Pory was in the region.
5. "Tlemmish" in the manuscript.

14

conduct Captain Argall his pinnace into Hudson's River,[6] put-
teth down in his plot a place some fifteen leagues to the west of
Elizabeth's Island, which he calleth Cod Island.[7]

And by the way, that you may know how strongly the Flemings make title from 40 to 44 degrees, they call Hudson his
river, "Prince Maurice his river"; Cape Cod, the "States Hooke";
Sagadahoc or thereabouts, "Prince Henricks river"; and the
great bay wherein Port Royal (taken by Captain Argall from the
French) was seated, "Grave Williams Bay."[8] And in the same
place they confine Virginia within the Cape Henry and Charles,
as if it had no further extension both north and south. Also, to
the south of Hudson's River, they name the country "*Aqua-
hanacke.*"[9]

Besides that plantation of New Plymouth in 41 degrees and
one half, and that other in Massachusetts[10] in 42 or thereabouts,
there is a third in Canada at Damerill's Cove[11] in 43 and 45 minutes, at the cost of Sir Ferdinando Gorges, consisting of some
thirteen persons, who are to provide fish all the year with a
couple of shallops for the most timely loading of a ship, and to
keep that island to be farmed out in Sir Ferninando's name to
such as shall there fish. And lest the French or the savages should

6. In 1622, the Council for New England made Sir Samuel Argall its "Admiral"
with the duty of excluding unlicensed operators from the Council's territory, North
America from 40° to 48°. American Antiquarian Society, *Proceedings*, Apr. 1867,
66–83.

7. Possibly an illusion, possibly Block Island. It appears as *Cabeleaus Eyleut* (?) on
the "Carte Figurative" (1616), reproduced in T. A. Janvier, *The Dutch Founding of
New York* (1903), between pages 20 and 21.

8. Pory was mixed up. Boston Bay was *Graaf Hendrycks* Bay; Casco Bay (or sometimes the water between Cape Ann and Portsmouth, N. H.), *Graaf Willem's*; Port
Royal is now Annapolis Basin, Nova Scotia. The Dutch names in the text have been
left in the half-translated state in which Pory wrote them. In modern Dutch, "States
Hooke" would be *Staten Hoek*.

9. *Aquamachukes* on the "Figurative Map" (1616), *Aquauachuques* on map by
Vander Donck (1656), reproduced in J. Winsor (ed.), *Narrative and Critical History
of America* (1884), IV, 433, 438.

10. Weston's rowdy crew at Wessagussett.

11. Damariscove Island, off Boothbay, Me.

root them out in winter, they have fortified themselves with a
strong palisado of spruce trees of some ten foot high, having
besides their small shot one piece of ordnance and some ten
good dogs.

Howsoever they speed, they undertake an hazardous attempt,
considering the savages have been this year, as those to the
north use to be by the French, furnished (in exchange of skins)
by some unworthy people of our nation with pieces, shot, powder, swords, blades and most deadly arrow heads; and with shallops from the French, which they can manage as well as any
Christian, as also their pieces, it being an ordinary thing with
them to hit a bird flying. And how little they are to be trusted
here as well as in Virginia, may appear by the killing lately of
the master of a ship of Plymouth[12] with eighteen of his company
among the islands toward the northeast, which was the cause
that the same ship lost her fishing voyage and went empty home.

Now, as concerning the soil, it is all along, as far as I could
perceive, rocky, rough and uneven; and, that as I hear, from a
little on this side [of] Cape Cod as far as to Newfoundland, being
all along the sea coast a labyrinth of innumerable islands or
broken lands rent in sunder by intricate channels, rivers and
arms of the sea. Upon these rocky grounds do grow naturally
fir, spruce, birch and other trees, and in some open places abundance of rasps, gooseberries, hurts[13] and such fruit; in other
places, high[14] rank grass for the grazing of cattle, to make hay
withal; as likewise, great plenty of pease like our English pease,
growing naturally without any tilth. Upon these rocky places,
there is passing good soil, yet culturable with hoe and spade
rather than with the plow. Yet they say that up the river Prina-
quie[15] there is a place of even champian[16] country without any

12. Plymouth, England.   13. Huckleberries.
14. "Hugh" in the manuscript.
15. This river is not identifiable. It may be an error in copying "Pentagoet," the
French name for the Penobscot.
16. Flat, open.

rocks, abounding with variety of excellent timber, and like at
Anquam[17] nearer unto Cape Ann,[18] a level of more beauty and
largeness.

Within an infinity of rocks may be intombed abundance of
rich minerals, among which silver and copper are supposed to
be the chief. Out of these rocks do gush out delicate streams of
water which, together with the temper of the air, maketh this
place marvelous wholesome in summer—which is the cause I
have not known one man sick all the time I was there, save only
that villain which accused you falsely concerning Swabber, and
died (aboard the *Bona Nova*) as he had lived, frantic.[19] Yet is the
air too cold here for the summer, but with an easterly wind subject to fogs and mists.

The people[20] seem to be of one race with those in Virginia,
both in respect of their qualities and language. They are great
lovers of their children and people, and very revengeful of
wrongs offered. They make their canoes, their arrows, their
bows, their tobacco pipes and other their implements far more
neat and artificially than in those parts. They dress, also, and
paint leather; and make trousers, buskins, shoes with far greater
curiosity. Corn they set none in their parts toward the north,
and that is the cause why Indian corn, pease and such like is the
best truck[21] for their skins—and then in winter especially, when
hunger doth most pinch them, which is the season when the
French do use to trade with them. They have the same names of
numbers with them in the south. *Accamus* (in the southern language, a dog) they call here *Aramouse*. For *Malta* (no), they pro-
nounce *Madda*; for *Matcheray* (nought), *Mathat*; for *Mitchin* (to
eat), *Mitterim*; for *Kijos* (the sun), *Hijos*; and many other like or

17. Gloucester or Annisquam.
18. "Anna" in the manuscript.
19. The *Bona Nova* was a ship often employed in the Virginia trade. Nothing
further is known about Swabber and the dead man.
20. Indians.
21. Goods for barter.

self-same words spoken by the rebels[22] of the South Colony. Neither is their manner of singing and dancing much different. Their babes here also they bind to a board and set them up against a wall, as they do here in the south. Likewise, their head they anoint with oil mixed with vermillion; and are of the same hair, eyes and skin that those are of.

22. Indians who performed the massacre of 1622 in Virginia.

EMMANUEL ALTHAM

Emmanuel Altham (1600-1635/1636)

EMMANUEL ALTHAM was born a gentleman, though his family had its connections with commerce and the legal profession rather than the titled aristocracy. His two older brothers successively held the family's country seat at Mark Hall, Latton, about twenty miles north of London. As a younger son, Altham inherited little of his parents' wealth and so, over objections by his relatives, sought excitement and his fortune in the expanding world of English overseas trade. Altham began as an investor in the Company of Adventurers for New Plymouth, served for a time as agent of the Company, and became an admirer of the colonists and New England with such ardor that he could more easily envision the colony's future success than see the hardships which the planters were enduring when he first arrived. He went to the New World with a sense of honor, moreover, rather than the qualities of a hard-driving trader. Perhaps he was not a typical Adventurer: his devotion to the cause of colonization and taste for the heroic side of commerce rather than the ledger went beyond the ordinary, and helped keep English backing for the Pilgrim plantation alive when profit did not.

Altham crossed the Atlantic to Plymouth the first time in the summer of 1623. He went as "Captain" of the *Little James* (James Bridge, master), the pinnace of about 44 tons which the Company was sending to the plantation for use in fishing and fur-trading expeditions. In 1623, the expert in charge of sailing a ship was her "master," and if there was a captain, he had command over the military and mercantile affairs of the voyage. Since his ship carried authorization to operate as a privateer, Altham had the decision about taking prizes as well as the trans-

21

action of business. After a year in New England waters, described in the first three of Altham's letters printed here, he recrossed the ocean with the ship. She was seized for the satisfaction of debts to two of the Company's members, Thomas Fletcher and Thomas Goffe, who sent her (but not under Altham) on a second voyage in 1625.

Altham's fourth letter from New England describes the occasion of his second expedition, on his own. Evidently his hopes for a future with the colony faded, for he returned to England some time before July 1626 and soon afterwards began to look for employment as a soldier with the East India Company.

Through the influence of his brother, Sir Edward, he was sent to the Company's fort at Surat and spent over two years in exploits around the Indian Ocean. The East India Company's business was a mixture of trade and raid — competing with the Portuguese for control of port cities in India and the trade to which they gave access. The climax of these years, for Altham, was an expedition to Madagascar and Mozambique to intercept the fleet of caracks from Portugal.

After a visit to England in 1630, Altham returned to India a more important man: Factor and Captain of the fort at Armagon (now abandoned, at a place about sixty miles north of Madras), the Company's main post on the east side of India. He served the firm well, rebuilt the fortifications, and finally began to accumulate wealth. He expected to return to England permanently and live in style — had even begun to order paintings and fancy bedding, but died at Armagon in January, 1635/1636.

The originals of the letters of Emmanuel Altham to Sir Edward Altham belonged to Dr. Otto Fisher, of Detroit, who before his death generously consented to their first publication here. The letter of Altham to James Sherley has been published in Massachusetts Historical Society, *Proceedings*, XLIV, 182–189, from a transcript of the original in the English Public Records Office (Admiralty Court Misc., bundle 1142), with editorial comment and notes by J. F. Jameson.

Emmanuel Altham to Sir Edward Altham

September, 1623

Most loving and kind brother,

My promise doth put me in re-
membrance, with the first opportunity of a messenger,[1] to write
unto you. And if I were not by promise, yet that special nearness
that is between us obliges me to the same, for as I have always to
this time found your constant affections towards me, so have I,
and shall continually, acknowledge the same.

And now, loving brother, since I have undertaken a voyage
not altogether pleasing to some of my friends — and because of
my forwardness in the same, I may be taxed with many censures
— therefore, as it doth more nearly concern me, I will here lay
down not what my ear hath heard, but what I have with my eyes
seen to be true.

After our departure from the Cowes in the Isle of Wight, we
recovered our desired passage three months and one day after,
being the 5th of August, with many bitter a storm. And I have
learned by this voyage that God hath made the seas more for use
than pleasure, but I praise the Lord for his goodness that I never
had my health better. And likewise by the blessings of God, I
have and hope to learn that at sea which will prove for my extra-
ordinary advantage. But everyone hath a time, although some
sooner than others.

After our arrival in New England, we found all our plantation
in good health, and neither man, woman or child sick. And here,
likewise, we found the other ship set forth by the Company,[2]

---

1. Edward Winslow, who left Plymouth for England on the *Anne*, Sept. 10, 1623.
2. The other ship was the *Anne*, of 140 tons, William Peirce, master. The Company

23

who came from Portsmouth six days after us, and arrived here at
New England ten days before, with all her people well—as we
with our people did the like. And yet one good wife Jennings[3]
was brought abed of a son aboard our ship and was very well.
And then, we had an old woman in our ship about four score
years of age, which was in good health—and this I speak not as
needful to write of, but to show that God did give us our health
when we looked not for it, and to those, likewise, that had not
been well a year before on the shore.

And now to come more nearer to that I intend to write of, and
first of the situation of the place—I mean the plantation at Patuxet.[4] It is well situated upon a high hill close unto the seaside,
and very commodious for shipping to come unto them. In this
plantation is about twenty houses, four or five of which are very
fair and pleasant, and the rest (as time will serve) shall be made
better. And this town is in such manner that it makes a great
street between the houses, and at the upper end of the town
there is a strong fort, both by nature and art, with six pieces of
reasonable good artillery mounted thereon; in which fort is continual watch, so that no Indian can come near thereabouts but
he is presently seen. This town is paled round about with pale of
eight foot long, or thereabouts, and in the pale are three great
gates. Furthermore, here is belonging to the town six goats,
about fifty hogs and pigs, also divers hens. And lastly, the town
is furnished with a company of honest men, that do, in what lies
in them, to get profit to the adventurers.

And now to speak more at large of the country and what profit

---

of Adventurers for New Plymouth (sometimes called by variants of this name) was
the organization of merchants who helped finance the Plymouth settlement. They
"adventured" their money; the Pilgrims were "planters," although in modern esti-
mation they were more adventurous.

3. The only passenger known to have a name similar to Jennings was John Jenny,
who lived to be an important man in the Plymouth Colony. This woman may have
been one in his series of wives.

4. Indian name for Plymouth.

is to be raised here; and first, to speak of the fishing that is in this country. Indeed it is beyond belief, but I can assure you thus much: that if a man be well provided with all things necessary for to make a fishing voyage, he may easily make his voyage two for one.[5] But lest this should seem incredible to some, I will give you an instance of the same. Before we got hither to Patuxet, we had many fogs at sea, insomuch that we were driven to lie at hull and to take down all our sails—and so went to fishing. In one hour we got 100 great cod, and if we would have but stayed after the fog broke up, we might quickly [have] loaded our ship —and, I am persuaded, had we been prepared with all things necessary for a fishing voyage, we might have loaded our ship in a week. I think we got 1000 in all. And indeed, when we had nothing else to do, my people took delight to catch them, although we threw them away again, as I think we did 300. One fish we got, I think, weighed 100 pound: it was as big a cod as ever was seen. We got many turbots, likewise, and one turbot we got gave all our ship a meal and to spare. And to speak what voyages of fishing hath been found and made this year, here hath been at Monhegan, Damerill's Cove, Anquam, Pemaquid, Sagadahoc, and the Isles of Shoals[6]—all principal places for fishing —about 400 sail. And every one of them, by their confession, say that they have made good voyages, and now most of them are gone into Spain, to sell their fish where they have ready gold for it.

And now to speak what sorts of other fish are here to be had. Here are great store of sturgeon—I mean abundance; likewise great of salmon, bass, trout, eels—and lobsters such infinite that when we have them the very multitude of them cloys us. There are likewise great store of other fish which I cannot remember, as clams and oysters.

5. Double his money.
6. Monhegan and Damerill's Cove (Damariscove) are islands off the coast of Maine, each with a well-protected small harbor. Pemaquid is the peninsula east of Boothbay, Me.; Sagadahoc is the extension of the Kennebec River below its junction with the Androscoggin. Anquam is Gloucester or Annisquam on Cape Ann, Mass. The Isles of Shoals are off New Hampshire.

And now to speak somewhat of our store of beaver's skins that are round about us both to the norward and southward. And now at this present, we are going to the southward into Hudson's River, where the Dutchmen have all their skins of the savages. We hope there to get good store of beaver's, otter's and martin's skins, as also fox skins and raccoon skins—all which will yield money good store in England. And towards Christmas we are to return to our plantation again. And then, before the fishermen come in February to the norward, we mean to go trade for all the skins that are to be had thereabout, and then to take the best stage for fishing in the country, and so to fish in the beginning of the year;[7] and then about May, 1624, to go trading for furs again. And then it may be so, that we will come home about Christmas come twelvemonth, but look not for me before I come. Divers occasions of employments may fall out so that I may be hindered —and indeed, I shall not desire to come for England unless I bring good store of profit with me, which I make no doubt of, by God's help.

Thirdly, I will speak somewhat of the timber in the country, which will raise great profit to the Adventurers. We have here as good timber as ever I saw—of many sorts. We have here cedar, beech, pine, oak, and divers other sorts, of which we have here sent a sample of about two or three hundred pounds worth, and with it a good many beaver's skins and furs of divers sorts.

Fourthly, we will say somewhat of the sarsaparilla and sassa-fras—as also, alkermes berries[8]—all which are worth good store

7. A fishing stage, built over rock ledges near some convenient harbor, was a scaffold or "wharf built of spruce trees, boards, and beach stones where the fish could be cleaned," salted and cured in the sun. The fishermen raced from Europe to get the best places, so a ship already in New England waters could hope to beat them all. S. E. Morison, *The Story of the "Old Colony" of New Plymouth* (1956), 122. The new year began on March 25 in the Old Style dating system.

8. "Alcerme" in the manuscript. Both Altham and Capt. John Smith believed that alkermes berries existed in North America. Perhaps they thought cranberries were the same things. Actually, alkermes berries are insects (species *eoccus ilicis*) which live in the bark of the kerm oak, a tree found around the Mediterranean Sea. The

of money in England, and of which, when I come myself, God willing, I will bring a pattern to London. For when I was at London, sarsaparilla was of two shillings a pound, at the least, and we have here enough to load a ship.

Fifthly, to speak of the profit that may arise by salt—and I make no doubt we shall make much salt before I come for England. And if we could but have salt to sell to the fishing ships that come hither yearly, I think we might compare our plantation to the Spaniards' Indies. And we have good hopes of making salt about a mile from our plantation, and it shall be put in execution 'ere long.[9]

Sixthly and lastly, here are many other things in this country to raise profit, as for example, at the place whereto we are now bound with our ship to the southward—the place is called Capawack[10]—there is a mountain of bole armeniac[11] and divers other metals. No English hath been there, but only one Captain Dermer whom was killed by the savages there;[12] for the savages in this place are very strong and are men of very able bodies. But notwithstanding, we mean to put it upon trial and to go well armed among them. We hope there to get store of skins.

And now, having spoken what is but the truth concerning the

pregnant females have a bright red color, and juice squeezed from them was used as a dye and a cordial, especially in times when they were still thought to be a vegetable.

9. A master salter went over on the *Anne*, but he proved a better talker than practitioner of his business. The Pilgrims gave him a lot of help, but he made no salt. In spite of the logic of the idea, saltmaking never became important in the Plymouth Colony.

10. Martha's Vineyard, Mass.

11. "Bowle alminact" in the manuscript. The term had many variants, but referred to an astringent earth found in Armenia, used as a styptic.

12. Capt. Thomas Dermer made two voyages of exploration along the Atlantic coast between Monhegan and Virginia in 1619 and 1620, employed by Sir Ferdinando Gorges and others interested in developing New England. He learned much and tried to establish peace with the Indians, but in his dealings with those near Narragansett Bay (where he liberated some French mariners) and Martha's Vineyard, he may have stirred up fear of the English. He was mortally wounded in a fight with Epenow, an Indian who had once been a captive of Sir Ferdinando and shown off as a curiosity in England. W. F. Gookin, *Capawack alias Martha's Vineyard*, 14–17.

profit that may with small labor be got for the Company of Adventurers, I will now, as briefly as I can, show you what good will redound to those that live here. And first, of the fish in the country, which, as I said before, is of all sorts in infinite number; and two, for the fowl that are in the country. Here are eagles of many sorts, pigeons, innumerable turkeys, geese, swans, duck, teel, partridge divers sorts, and many others fowl, [so] that one man at six shoots hath killed 400. And then to speak of the healthfulness of the air. It lieth in 42 degrees of northerly latitude. We have here the wind come off the land all the day time, and in the night off the sea, which is wondrous wholesome. Some few have had agues at the first coming over, but not sick above a week—and myself was ill for three or four days, but I thank these good friends of mine at the plantation, I am recovered pretty well, thanks be to God. Thirdly, those that live here need never want wood, for here is great store. Four (fourthly), here is as good ground as ever I heard of, whenas the ground yield five or six hundred for one—nay, some 1400![13] And this year they have great store of corn—as goodly corn as ever I saw —of which I have sent you six ears. And if God will, when I come myself, you nor my worshipful friend, Sir John Leventhorpe, shall not want so much beaver's skins as will make each of you a hat. But to our purpose, I say that none of these commodities can be got without a little pains, and the most pains and cost is to be stowed at the beginning; for men must provide for the worst, that they may have provision for themselves a twelvemonth if these things fail—and then the[y] must take pains to build them houses and the like. And because I have spoken somewhat large of the country—and indeed I have good cause, because if I were well provided with all things necessary, as servants and the like, I could live here contentedly with great pleasure—but I shall better think and determine of such matters when more important business doth not call me aside.

13. This is not impossible with Indian corn, but exceedingly unlikely.

And now I will speak somewhat of the savages in the country about—I mean the native Indians. The nearest that any dwell unto [Plymouth] is fourteen miles, and their town is called Manomet. Only without our pales dwells one Hobomok, his wives and his household (above ten persons), who is our friend and interpreter, and one whom we have found faithful and trusty. He I carry away with me to the southward. And now, likewise, in this bay wherein we live, in former time hath lived about 2000 Indians. Here is not one living now, nor not one living which belonged to this plantation before we came, so that the ground on which we are planted belongs to nobody.[14]

And now to speak of the king of the country, who is a great emperor among his people. Upon the occasion of the Governor's marriage,[15] since I came, Massasoit was sent for to the wedding, where came with him his wife, the queen, although he hath five wives. With him came four other kings and about six score men with their bows and arrows—where, when they came to our town, we saluted them with the shooting off of many muskets and training our men. And so all the bows and arrows was brought into the Governor's house, and he brought the Governor three or four bucks and a turkey. And so we had very good pastime in seeing them dance, which is in such manner, with such a noise that you would wonder. And at that time when we gave Massasoit his hat, coat, band and feather, I craved a boy of him for you, but he would not part with him; but I will bring you one hereafter.

And now to say somewhat of the great cheer we had at the Governor's marriage. We had about twelve pasty venisons, besides others, pieces of roasted venison and other such good cheer in such quantity that I could wish you some of our share.

14. Hobomok was a Wampanoag, from west of Plymouth; Squanto, the last of the Indians formerly living around Patuxet, had died in 1622.
15. William Bradford married his second wife, Alice, daughter of Alexander Carpenter, widow of Edward Southworth, Aug. 14, 1623.

For here we have the best grapes that ever you say[16]—and the biggest, and divers sorts of plums and nuts which our business will not suffer us to look for.

And now to speak somewhat of Massasoit's stature. He is as proper a man as ever was seen in this country, and very courageous. He is very subtle for a savage, and he goes like the rest of his men, all naked but only a black wolf skin he wears upon his shoulder. And about the breadth of a span he wears beads about his middle. And these beads they make themselves, which they account as gold above silver before the beads we bring out of England.

Lastly, to speak a little in what peace and friendship we are with the savages, which peace we have had with Massasoit ever since our coming. And he never expressed his love more to us than of late; for in the Massachusetts there was a colony—I may rather say a company of idle persons, for they had no civil government among themselves, much less were they able to govern and rule Indians by them. And this plantation was begun about one year and one half since by one Mr. Weston,[17] who came this year to see his plantation. But by many notorious deeds among themselves, and also having in their necessity stolen corn from the Indians, the Indians began to condemn them and would have killed all the English, but they feared that when the English of Patuxet did hear what they had done, then they would set upon the squaw sachem in the Massachusetts and so kill all the

16. Saw. "Say" is an obsolete equivalent.

17. Thomas Weston, the London merchant who originally promoted the Company of Adventurers for New Plymouth in 1620. He wanted profit from the business and, when his patience wore thin with a complete settlement, sent out the private all-male colony which Altham here refers to. Without family considerations, the men were expected to stick to money-making activities like trade with the Indians and grow food for themselves in their spare time. The colony was planted at Wessagusset in present Weymouth, Mass., after sixty or so "lusty men" had lived at the charge of the Pilgrims during the summer of 1622. Weston was devoted to America as well as profit and shady deals, though, and went to Virginia and Maryland as a planter for several years before dying in England, deep in debt. C. M. Andrews, *Colonial Period of American History* (1934), I, 261–265, 330–331.

Indians in the Massachusetts. Whereupon they determined another resolution: to cut the English at Patuxet, whom they stand in fear of now, and the English at Massachusetts both at one time. But in the mean time, the great Massasoit sent to Patuxet for some physic, because he was fallen very sick, and so, by God's help, he was cured. And upon his recovery, he made known the plot of the Indians of Massachusetts against us, and told us that if we would not go fight with them, he would. So at the return of our surgeon from Massasoit, came a messenger from Mr. Weston's plantation at Massachusetts, telling us that there was a plot against us by the Indians of Massachusetts. Whereupon the Governor, Mr. William Bradford (well worthy the place), sent Captain Standish with some six or seven others to the Massachusetts to bring away the head of him that made the broil. And so, by God's goodness, he killed our chief enemy and five or six others without any hurt to our part, and brought away the head of the chiefest of them.[18] And [it] is set on the top of our fort, and instead of an ancient,[19] we have a piece of linen cloth dyed in the same Indian's blood, which was hung out upon the fort when Massasoit was here. And now the Indians are most of them fled from us, but they now seek to us to make peace. But we are informed by Hobomok that eight shallops of Indians, well provided, are coming this way. They say themselves that they come to fight with other Indians that have killed

18. Capt. Standish and his company went to the Wessagusset settlement to warn the men of the conspiracy. After days of cautious waiting and veiled exchange of threats with some of the leading Massachusetts Indians, Standish got four of them into a room with about an equal number of his men and assassinated three, including Pecksuot and Wituwamat, whose head he took to Plymouth. In other ambuscades, with some aid by Weston's men, the Pilgrim expeditionary force killed several others. The Wessagusset settlers, who had been reduced to great want and dependence on the Indians, abandoned their place, most going to the Maine coast to work for the fishermen and get passage back to England. The story is told most fully in Edward Winslow, "Winslow's Relation," in Young (ed.), *Chronicles of the Pilgrim Fathers* ("Everyman's Library," 1936), 313-332, or some other edition of Winslow's *Good News from New England.*

19. Flag.

a friend of theirs, but if they come at us to offer any violence, I doubt they will never carry their shallops back again—it may be, not with their lives. And these Indians, we hear, have muskets and fowling pieces, with powder and shot, which they have bought of the Frenchmen in Canada and of the Englishmen at the Isle of Monhegan; but that trade is already stopped by the King's proclamations concerning the same trade.

And now, loving brother, I have little else to write of unto you—but only one thing I thank you kindly for, and that was for the last letter you sent me in England, wherein you desire [me] to hold fast to the truth and likewise to be diligent in my place. Of both which make no doubt—no! be persuaded that I will rather die a thousand deaths than once to shame God or my country. And now, seeing that I am entered into this place, doubt not but that I will always increase in knowledge. And indeed, when I undertook this voyage at first, I always held the art of navigation to be most hard and difficult, but now, through some practice and reading, I have attained to that I hope never to forget. And I hope by that time I see old England to be able to conduct a ship myself, safe into any harbor in New England. But God disposeth of all things. And truly, I never lived better to my content nor among those who can more respect me as the Company in old England and here[20] likewise do, who think nothing too good for me. I praise God, I have my health 'till now that I wrote this letter—but I mended apace.

And now, loving brother, I must make an end, although I think no pains sufficient to express my love unto you. I doubt not but you will show yourself a friend to me in taking care for that little stock I have. I am desirous it should increase—and in your hands, if you think it profitable to you. I know you will deal the more providently for me, because of divers reasons well

---

20. Adventurers and Planters were both members of the Company under the terms of the agreement made in 1620. Settlers were accounted as having put in the value of a £10 share.

known to yourself. I pray let that same £100 be taken of my
Mr. Hawes or his heirs when it is due (and that will be about
March, 1624), and if you and my brother Hawtry[21] think good,
take it into your own hands. I have wrote to my brother Hawtry
to buy me the books of English voyages, which will do me great
good. I pray look that they be bought me, and send by this messenger that is come from New England and hath lived there
three years. And he comes away about December from London,
that he may come with the fishermen, to be here in February. I
pray let those books be of the same voyages that is lately put
forth by Mr. Purchas, minister about Ludgate.[22]

Thus much I have thought good to let you understand concerning the estate of myself and New England, and now I will
take my leave of you, desiring the God of hosts to guide you and
yours in your going out and coming, so that all your labors may
prosper under your hands, and that your life in this world of
misery may be such a life that may prepare you to a better in the
world to come.

And thus, my kindest love and best affections being remembered to you, desiring you to accept of this mite (being compared to my mind). Likewise, as I am bound to respect, so let
my love be remembered to my sister your wife, and to my worthy
friend, Sir John Leventhorpe, and to his good lady, and all the
rest of that noble house, as to my Lady Fowle and Sir John
Fowle, my brother Thomas, and my sister Mary.[23] And I pray
merrily tell her it will be no tarrying for me because I know not
when I shall come into England. But I pray likewise tell [her]
that I could here give her much land if she will come and live

21. Ralph Hawtry, husband of Altham's sister Mary.
22. Samuel Purchas, *Hakluytus Posthumus or Purchas His Pilgrimes* (London,
1625), 4 vol. The books had been announced as early as 1621.
23. The Leventhorpes were neighbors and close friends of the Althams. Sir Edward Altham married one of Sir John's daughters. Sir John Fowle had married another daughter. "My brother Thomas" was the son and heir of Sir John Leventhorpe.
Mary Leventhorpe was another daughter.

among this wild scene of Indians. I hope this will make her smile.
And now, I pray let my love be remembered to my aunt Wolley,
hoping that she will have me in her mind, although not in her
eye; I mean I hope she will remember me at her death, which
must be one day.[24] Pray remember me likewise to Mr. Denn and
his wife and old goodwife Stracy, and to my worthy Adventurer
Henry Stracy, who, if he claims his money, let him have it, I
pray you, for I see it will come in with profit. Pray likewise remember my love to Mr. Bland and William Watson, and pray
tell them thus much: that because a ship could not be got when
I had cattle in my hands, and likewise because I could get nobody
to join with me, I put that money into the common stock; and it
shall be answered in that, which, if they be not contented, I will
repay again. The like, I pray, do to goodman Wells. Remember
me to him and tell him I find great need of his cousin, the potter.[25]
I pray, sir, let them read this letter—either the same or a copy
of the same—and so, likewise, I pray let my noble friend, Sir
John Leventhorpe; although I have wrote to him, yet I refer him
to particulars in your letters.

And so I take my leave of you; but I pray remember me to my
father Adee and mother Adee, and to all the rest of my friends to
whom I am by any way tied—as to Seth Haggar and Edward
Skoles, whose so long continuance and good service in your
house have caused me to speak well of them.

And thus I end, desiring the Lord to direct you in all your
ways, words and actions, and to guide you by his Holy Spirit
and so to enable you, that in what you have been wanting to
glorify his name in this world among men, your heart may be
more and more touched with the reverence of so great a God,
and to labor more and more to glorify him here, that so you may

24. Margaret Wolley at least had him in her will, proved in 1635, eight months before Altham's death.
25. Mr. Denn was rector in Latton, a man of Puritanical leanings. Stracy was a
tenant of the Althams; Mr. Bland, a minister and family friend; Watson, a London
gunsmith; Wells, a tenant of the Althams.

be glorified by him in the world to come, where one day, if I see you not in this world, I make no doubt but to meet you, which God, for Christ Jesus' sake grant unto us. And so I bid you, Farewell! Farewell in the Lord; and the God of heaven, earth, seas and all things be with you and protect you in your going forth and coming in. And so, being guided and directed by God's holy angels, you may not be ashamed to show yourself before God and the Lord Christ at that great day of account when all things shall be made known. And so, even from my heart and soul, I take my leave of you and the rest of my other friends who are mentioned in my other letters. *Vale!*

I shall be glad to hear from you. In the beginning of December, pray send your letters to Mr. Sherley's in Crooked Lane.[26] Divers matters I could write, but only this let me tell you: that I would entreat you to stir up a few friends to venture four or five hundred pounds with me when I come myself. For I then intend to make a voyage to fish, which I make no doubt but I can get two of one in eight months. This thing I thought good to impart to you, and do entreat you to provide such a course against I come home, if you can.

Forth, this is a most ordinary voyage undertaken.

Thus I rest,

your most loving brother,

EMMANUEL ALTHAM.

I have sent my sister Altham six ears of Indian corn and beans to sow in her garden. Also, I have sent you a tobacco pipe which I had of the Indians.

---

26. James Sherley, goldsmith and treasurer of the Company of Adventurers.

Emmanuel Altham to Sir Edward Altham

March, 1623/1624.

Loving and kind brother,

My love being remembered to you and the rest of my loving friends, these few words being caused by the fitness of a messenger, they are to let you understand that I am in good health and so have been a long time, as I hope also of you.

I have been upon a voyage to the southward of New England, where we have discovered many brave places where never any Christians were before. And this part of the country—I mean to the southward of New England—is far better land and more commodious places for situation than are in any part of this country besides.[1] For there is not only good ground in abundance, with excellent good timber, but here are great store of furs which now the Dutchmen get because our Company of New England have not sent by us so good trucking stuff as they should have, and so have disappointed themselves much. Insomuch that whereas we thought for to have got with our pinnace three or four hundred pounds worth of skins, we have now got small store, to my exceeding great grief.

But this is not all they have hindered themselves of, for in their plantation is the better half women and children, and divers of the rest are very unwilling, so that only the burden of the plantation lieth on the shoulders of some few who are both honest, wise and careful.[2] And if it were not for them few, the

1. On this voyage, Altham went as far as the Narragansett Indians; that is, at least to western Rhode Island of today.
2. Before experience showed the falsity of the idea, promoters of colonies in Amer-

plantation would fall, and come to nothing—yea, long before this time; and it is so much the more likely because that now by a sudden fire one half of the plantation was burnt down by fire, upon the 5th of November last, wherein was burnt and spoiled the goods of all such that came this last time into New England and are now by reason of this loss forced to come again for England.[3]

But, although it hath pleased God to lay his heavy hand on these poor people and plantation, yet the fault is neither in some of the planters here nor in the unfruitfulness of the country. For I assure thus much: that a better country was never seen nor heard of, for here are a multitude of God's blessings; but they are not to be enjoyed by idle people that think to have all things at wishing for. But if men will take pains at first, they may live afterwards bravely. Indeed, in this country is no clothes to be had, nor divers other things which a man may make a good shift without. Yea, here is all things to be had to a contented mind; and it is not for men to live here that think of their former prosperity

---

ica thought of the settlements as glorified trading posts. This plan did work in Asia and logically ought to have in America if, as men like Altham or other Adventurers thought, profit was to be gained by trade and farming be only a spare-time adjunct.

3. Not all went back. Nor was the damage so great; three or four houses burned down. The common store house and its contents were saved by means of good organization and wet cloths, although the fire started in an adjoining shed. Bradford said the blaze was started by some sailors from a ship in the service of the Council for New England. The men, who wanted a cheerful atmosphere for a carousal, built a big fire which may have gone out of control. Evidence also turned up to show that the storehouse was deliberately lit. Bradford, *Of Plymouth Plantation*, 136–137.

Furthermore, the town was more than restored quite soon. Captain John Smith printed a description of Plymouth in 1624 which, in addition to information about the government and economy of the settlement, reported that "At New Plymouth is about 180 persons, some cattle and goats, but many swine and poultry; thirty-two dwelling houses, whereof seven were burnt the last winter, and the value of five hundred pounds in other goods. The town is impaled about half a mile in compass. In the town upon a high mount they have a fort well built with wood, loam and stone, where is planted their ordnance; also a fair watchtower, partly framed, for the sentinel." This passage, in original spelling, may be found in "Generall Historie of Virginia, New England, and the Summer Isles," edition of 1624, reprinted in Edward Arber and A. G. Bradley (eds.), *Travels and Works of Captain John Smith* (1910), II, 782.

and company—friends and kinsfolk, but it is good for such that resolve to forget and leave all these things for a time, and do labor as they think to live by it hereafter.

Neither can I speak but well of the profits that are to be raised here by fishing—indeed, it is such that you would admire. But the best actions whatsoever, being badly undertaken, come to little or no effect. So this plantation, being undertaken by men unexperienced in plantations, is like to feel the smart of it. And also, how is it possible that those men that never saw fishing in their lives should raise profit by fishing? And if they had known it never so well, yet if they had not [been] able of body, they could not perform any matter; for how shall women and children do men's labors? The reason, in conclusion: this I say to you, that unless some other means be taken, which to do is impossible, no means of profit can be raised to the Adventurers for their money again.

If any man thinks to adventure money to have land, this I tell thee: that if they will give me a very small matter, I will make sure to them 10,000 acres of as good land as any in England. And this I am sure of. But although at this time I do fully declare to you the estate of this plantation, yet I pray conceal it 'till others have reported the like. And although these matters may seem strange to you, in regard of the ample relations that have been made in the praise of this plantation, yet take it no otherwise than thus: that it hath been the Company's fault in England, who have sent over so many helpless people that the Governor here (who is a wise gentleman) will not entertain some of them. And secondly, their fault hath been that the planters here have not had good trucking stuff to please the Indians. Indeed, no question, if we had commodity, we might have skins great store. And now I hope this is apparent to you, that the fault is not in the country, which is so good that if my ability would reach, I would settle some plantation—and yet, I hope I would not over-reach myself with hopes—but until that time I do resolve, if I can conveniently, to come hither a-fishing yearly, if God bless me homewards. And I do not doubt but to do the like that other men do, for other ships that come the last year (and this year) have got more fish than their ships could carry; and so carry it for Spain and sell it for great rates. But of this hereafter, if God bless me now home.

Indeed, the Lord hath preserved me miraculously. For, coming to anchor by a great many sands, when it was little wind, it proved at last great store of wind and a great storm, insomuch that our anchors came home and almost laid us upon the sands. And the storm increasing, we were fain to cut our mainmast overboard, and had much ado to save our lives in our ship. But thanks be to God, we were saved and our ship, and are at this time in a good harbor at Patuxet,[4] blessed be God! And here in this harbor we are to stay this winter, for this country is subject to wonderful storms in the winter time; and here it is very cold weather. Yet we have very poor fare here all this winter, being cold water[5] and beef, sometimes, because we have but little of it; and now and then we have good store of fowl. But for all these crosses and disheartenings, I was never better nor better contented in my life, which I thank God for, for I know it cannot be mended with wishes and wailings.

Thus much have I declared unto you concerning our plantation, entreating you to keep it close from the Company and not to think the worse of this country, in which nature hath almost emptied herself to replenish it. And although our beginning is bad, yet I hope that the fishing voyage I am now bound out upon will bring somewhat to the Adventurers, and also enable my own judgment to undertake the like for myself, if God prosper me now. Indeed, if the making of salt here did not require a greater

4. Plymouth. The ship was anchored outside Plymouth harbor when the storm blew up and almost drove her on the flats called Brown's Islands.

5. Englishmen of the seventeenth century thought life barely possible without beer.

charge of money from the Company, it would do well; but this
I say: that if salt be made here to reap store of profit, it requires
a greater charge than hath been laid out already, which I think
the Company will not disburse without seeing more hopes of
profit.

Thus entreating you not to expect me before I come, for when
it will be I know not—indeed, I do not desire to come before I
have made what profit I can to the Adventurers; which, if it may
not be, I have done my utmost and I hope they will accept of it.
In the mean time, my love and well wishes being remembered to
you, to my sister and to all your children, especially to my three
cousins, James, John and Leventhorpe.[6] I pray likewise remember my service to my most worthy and kind friend, Sir John
Leventhorpe and his Lady, to both whose services I acknowledge
myself bound many ways. Likewise, pray remember me to Sir
John Fowle and his Lady, and to my brother Thomas, and also
to my sister Mary, and to all the rest of that worthy stock. Also,
pray have my love remembered to Mr. Denn and his wife, and
also to Henry Stracy, goodman Watson, and Mr. Bland and
Thomas Wells.[7] And pray tell them that if they mislike their
adventure I have put into the Company for them, I will return
them their monies again; but I pray do you agree with them as
you will. I pray, good sir, be as a loving brother to me (which I
doubt not of) in increasing my little stock which, if God take me
away, may be the better for yours. But whether I live or die, you
shall never be the worse for it. Thus, loving, loving brother, have
I wrote in haste, entreating you to hold me excused if I have
done anything that might not seem worthy of your love. Thus
taking my leave of you, of the rest of my good friends, I bid you
farewell, entreating the Lord to be with you and to guide you in
your ways; that so, you having dealt honestly and conscionably
here, serving the Lord in truth and uprightness of heart, you

6. Altham's nephews, sons of Sir Edward.
7. See notes 21, 23, 25 to preceding letter.

may for the same be rewarded in the kingdom of heaven, where all tears and sorrows shall pass away; which God, for Christ's sake, grant unto us. Even so, Farewell, loving brother; and, if it be God's will, to send us once again to meet.

Your ever-loving and kind brother, till death,

EMMANUEL ALTHAM.

I pray remember my love to Edward Skoles and Seth Haggar.[8] And I pray let Edward Skoles know I would have wrote to him, but my leisure would not give me leave.

8. Old family servants. See preceding letter.

Emmanuel Altham to James Sherley

May, 1624.

Most worthy friends,

Your loving letters I have both received much about one time (being about the middle of April, 1624), wherein I conceive both your great love and care over me, which for my part shall never be rewarded with ingratitude. It pleased God that your ship called the *Charity* arrived at Plymouth in New England about five weeks after her departure from the English coast, but the certain day I know not, because I was at that time sixty leagues from thence at Pemaquid a-fishing. But after she had delivered her passengers and goods, she went immediately to Cape Ann, where, in all likelihoods, they are like to make a good voyage, if God withhold it not. For in all possibility, the settled course which yourself and the Company have taken will bring in much profit—for indeed, it is the only means above all other. Yet notwithstanding, the trade of furs may help, but that is not so sure a thing, by reason of divers (as I may call them) interlopers.

So soon as Mr. Peirce his coming into the land[1] came to my ears, I was forced much against my mind, both by the importunity of Mr. Bridge and insolences of all our company, to make a voyage from Pemaquid to Plymouth; which, had I not undertaken, although with much hazard of my person, all our company had and would have dispersed themselves. And if either myself or the master would detain them, they openly threatened a more speedy revenge: either to kill us or to blow our ship up. But these things are past, and the party dead who spake it, and

1. On the *Charity*.

42

I fear that God who knoweth all hearts, prevented him by death
from acting those villainous projects which, by his words in his
life, he professed to do.[2] The occasions of this was two: first, in
regard provisions went very hard with us, and the next was a
foolish and needless fear they had of their wages. To prevent all
this and farther mischief, I went to Plymouth about the beginning of April; where, by the way, I was forced with contrary
winds and foul weather to stay somewhat longer than I wished.
But at my coming to Cape Ann, I there found Mr. Winslow and
master Peirce,[3] for which I was very joyful. And so, having received of them divers commendations and letters from yourself
and my other friends, I went with all possible speed to Plymouth
to know the Governor's resolution. For thus it was, that provisions we had but very few before Christmas, but were fain to have
some pease out of Plymouth store.[4] And so, because we were
going to fish among our countrymen, we thought to get divers
things by reason of Mr. Bridge his acquaintance, but these our
hopes were much frustrated. For, coming to the fishermen, we
could have no provision without present pay, which I was desti-
tute of, notwithstanding I offered to become bond for anything
I took up. But they not regarding neither the Company's nor
my word did rather solicit our men to come work with them, for
their victuals, and to leave the ship, than to show any love or
friendship to us in helping us. Therefore, rather than our company should go away and our voyage be overthrown, we were

2. The troublemaker probably was one of the men drowned in the wreck of the
Little James (see below). The sailors of the pinnace, however, had been discontented
since early in the voyage. They believed they had signed on for privateering, to get
their pay in shares of prize ships. After a near mutiny at Plymouth, Gov. Bradford
helped arrange regular wages for them, and kept them on the ship for the exploration
of southern New England, but they still insisted that they would not go on a fishing
voyage. "A Letter of William Bradford and Isaac Allerton, 1623," *American Historical
Review*, VIII (1902–03), 296.

3. William Peirce was to be shipmaster of the *Charity* on her return voyage. Edward Winslow had returned from England on that ship.

4. In 1624 all goods in the general storehouse at Plymouth belonged to the Company.

constrained to use a present, though unwilling means[5] to get
some provision (as bread and pease) which before we were des-
titute of. So, having dispatched my business at Plymouth and
received my order from the Governor, Mr. Bradford, and his
Assistants, which was that look what fish we had caught in our
pinnace should presently be brought to Cape Ann and to deliver it to Mr. Peirce, and afterwards to aid and help Mr. Peirce
in his voyage, in what we could, both with our men and boats.
To all which, as I am in duty bound, so I consented unto it, and
with all convenient speed went away to our ship, Mr. Winslow
being with me.

And by this time, which was about the last of April, I thought
Mr. Bridge had killed about 10,000 fish, for more I think our
salt would not have saved; but by the backwardness of our people, and strange mishap, these hopes were quite altered. For,
coming within one day's journey of our ship, this untimely news
came to me that our pinnace was cast away and Mr. Bridge and
two of our men drowned, being John Vow and Peter Morrett.
All which news did not a little trouble me, knowing what great
cost and charge you have been at for us, and also knowing that
upon the good and prosperity of the ship and voyage depended
part of my reputation and profit. But this unwelcome news did,
in conceit, deprive of both. But coming home to our ship, I there
found this news true thus far: that Mr. Bridge, our master, was
drowned and the two men, and the ship in a very strange manner
spoiled. For thus it fortuned that upon the 10th of April, 1624,
happened a great storm, and some of our cables that we were
moored withal gave way and slip off on the place they were made
fast to ashore. And so, the wind and sea being very high, drave
our ship ashore upon rocks where she beat.[6] In the meantime,

5. Probably they took supplies from the trading post near the mouth of the Piscataqua River (near modern Portsmouth, N. H.) kept by David Thompson. In his will,
Altham left 40s. to a mistress Thomson in New England, presumably the man's
widow, as repayment of a debt she did not know of.

6. At Damariscove Island, off Maine. The harbor usually gave ships good protection in rough weather.

being night, the master and company arose, and every man shifted for themselves to save life; but the master going into his cabin to fetch his whistle, could not get into any boat about the ship, the sea brake so over the ship. And so by that means, before a boat could come, the ship overset and drowned him and the other two. And the rest, that were got into our shallops that hung about the ship, had much ado to recover the shore—your cousin, for one. For the ship oversetting, pitch her mainyard into one boat where were six or seven of our men, and so sunk her. For those that could then swim got to the shore with much hurt; the rest that could not swim were drowned. And so, before the next morning, our ship was quite under water sunk, and nothing to be seen save only the tops of her masts sometimes, for the sea did rake her to and fro upon the rocks. All which disasters did not a little trouble me, for our ship was not only spoiled, our men drowned, but we that were saved lost the most part of what we had in the ship. Myself, especially, lost my books and some clothes, and most of what I had. But my comfort is that God will restore me something one day again, for afflictions are but trials of his love. We lost three shallops, and our ship's boat and another shallop we borrowed which we[7]

After my coming to our ship and seeing how all things stood, and that although the ship were much spoiled and bruised— insomuch that some of our neighbors very dishonestly enticed our men to leave the ship and to seek out for their victuals, showing them that the ship was unrecoverable and using many arguments of disuasion to them, God knoweth, who were willing to entertain anything against us before, but now laying hold on of this opportunity rejoicing or[8] I here[9] departed. But at my coming home, I got them all together and sought far and near

7. "A sentence written lengthways in the margin, and not completed." J. F. Jameson, in Massachusetts Historical Society, *Proceedings*, XLIV, 184n.
8. 'Ere.
9. From Plymouth.

for help to recover our ship, if it were possible, which to do
seemed difficult. But by the help of one Mr. Cooke of Bastable[10]
and divers of his friends and my acquaintance, weighed her out
of the water, and so by the help of many hands we got the ship
into a place nearby, convenient to see what possibility there was
of saving the ship. So, having viewed her, there was broken of
her starboard side six or seven plank and some timbers, which
we mended with help; and on her larboard side, half her plank,
timbers and knees were broken in such sort that then she was
thought impossible to hold together, by reason of the hurt she
had received outward and the shaking of the beams and timbers
inwardly. But blessed be God, by the help and means that I have
got of carpenters, she is now made up as strong and sufficient
for the sea as ever she was.[11] And if not one of our company
come in her, yet by the help of God, we being fitted with a sufficient man master, I will come in her.

And do not doubt but, through God's mercies, to do well in
her, although for this time we shall not make so good a voyage as
is expected. For whereas we thought to have got ten or twelve
thousand fish, we had scarce one thousand, and some of that
was lost, and all our salt. For the ship being beat ashore, brake
down our stages, and there we lost both the salt and fish that was
in it. And all the rest of the salt, powder, provision, and many

10. Probably master of a fishing vessel from Barnstaple, Devonshire, England.
"Bastable," however, is to be found on Cape Ann on Capt. John Smith's map of New
England (1614 and later versions), and there were more or less permanent residents
on Cape Ann by 1624.

11. Bradford, who wrote over twenty years after the event, remembered the salvage
episode as though Altham had not been involved: ". . . some of the fishing masters
said it was a pity so fine a vessel should be lost and sent them [i.e., the Plymouth set-
tlers] word that if they would be at the cost, they would both direct them how to
weigh her and let them have their carpenters to mend her. They thanked them and
sent men about it, and beaver to defray the charge, without which all had been in
vain. So they got coopers to trim I know not how many tun of cask, and being made
tight and fastened to her at low water, they buoyed her up; and then with many
hands hauled her on shore in a convenient place where she might be wrought upon.
And then hired sundry carpenters to work upon her, and other to saw plank, and at
last fitted her and got her home." Bradford, *Of Plymouth Plantation*, 163.

other things (which, if God spare my life, I will give account of)
were lost. The rest of the things that we saved shall safely and
truly be delivered by me to you, with an account of all our men's
carriages and behaviors, that so you may reward some and re-
prove others.

And now, loving sir, since that I have troubled you with writing thus far, pardon me if I be too tedious; for it makes me continually be the more larger to you in writing, because I know
both you and many other good men have laid out much money
upon Plymouth plantation, and especially as for the goods upon
this ship. So do I conceive and know your eyes are upon us in a
more especial manner. And for that this voyage hath not begun
nor ended so well as either you or I could wish, yet I pray pardon me for a while in the same, until I shall come to speak with
you and the rest of the Company. For until then, I will neither
commend my care and diligence, nor discommend the want of
either of them, for full soon may a man err. But as my labor and
care was never wanting heretofore, so, until I shall make a full
accomplishment of this troublesome voyage and then to deliver
all things into your own hand, I will continue the same. And as
at this time I have no man to assist me that I can trust (the master being gone), so will I strain to the uttermost of my knowledge
to bring everything to the same order it was, and then to come
for England, if our Governor pleaseth. And he hath sent me
word that he will provide me a sufficient man for master, notwithstanding Richard Gardiner[12] hath earnestly requested it,
claiming it as his due by place, but some say not by sufficiency.
I will say no more concerning him because I know you shall understand it by others; only thus much I must needs say: that so
far as he could, he was willing to help us with the ship. And now
he takes it somewhat unkindly that, seeing the Company have
sent our ship's company assurance for their wages, that he is not

12. One of the passengers on the *Mayflower*, "Richard Gardiner became a seaman
and died in England or at sea." Bradford, *Of Plymouth Plantation*, 447.

intimated therein. So much for that, which is to be left to your and the Company's wisdom.

And once again let me be pardoned if I seem to be overbold. I understand by your letter to Mr. Bridge that you are somewhat discontented with me for not taking a Frenchman which we met withal; but to the contrary, wonderfully commend and extol Mr. Bridge for his courage and forwardness in the same, notwithstanding my backwardness. To answer which, I will do in few words. It so happened that about 400 leagues off the Lands End of England, we met with a small Frenchman. As I take it, he was of Rochelle.[13] In the morning we had sight one of another and he stood right with us and we with him. Coming near us, he spied us to be an Englishman, so he stood away from us and by a sudden puff of wind brake his mainmast. For we being desirous to hear news and also to see if he had any skins aboard or if he had been a-trading on the coast of New England, we stood after him and hailed him what he was and whence for. He told us he was of Rochelle and that he had but 7000 of cor-fish[14] aboard of him and that he was come from the Bank of Newfoundland a-fishing; and also that his ship was leaky, so he made the more haste home before he had made his voyage. But we mistrusting him, sent our boat aboard him to see if he had skins, but in conclusion we saw he was very poor and had not been ashore on no place; and so gave us some fish which at that time we stood in great need of as also of wood (of which he had none because he had not been on land nowhere). All these things being consid-

13. La Rochelle. This meant that the ship was owned and manned by French Protestants. La Rochelle was a Huguenot stronghold under the Edict of Nantes and became the center of resistance to royal attempts to revise the privileges of Protestants. English public opinion backed the Huguenots and tended to regard the people of La Rochelle as partners in an international religious struggle. When it came to national rights over trade, however, French Protestants were to be treated as foreigners, though with more consideration than Catholics.

14. Codfish "caught close to shore, landed within a couple of days, and lightly salted and cured largely in the sun." Morison, *Story of the "Old Colony" of New Plymouth*, 122.

ered, I hope you will not blame me, for I would do in your behalf
in that kind rather more than less than my commission would
bear me out in. But this ship was 500 leagues from any part of
New England when we met her and if I should have done it, I
had brought a great trouble both upon you and myself. For I will
assure you and all the Company that if you will but get a letter of
mart[15] and a safe protection from His Majesty of England for
taking of Frenchmen on Newfoundland Bank, you might easily
with this pinnace take and leave what ships you list. For we had
sight of twenty sail of Frenchmen at one time, and I believe never
a one had any ordnance. But to end, pray pardon me if I have
done amiss, but what I did, I have done (in my opinion and in
the opinion of all the companies at Plymouth) for your peace
and my own safety. For the Governor hath seen my commission
and saith, himself, I could not have answered it. Therefore, pray
blame me not for my good will and care, for I should be very loth
to lose a friend for nothing and upon no occasion, especially
when friends are hard to get. And as at this time, although I
might complain of my time all spent because it hath been a
troublesome time to me, yet I am quite of another mind; for as I
was called by God to this place, so, through his blessing, I will
discharge it honestly, whether I lose or get by it.

But out of all question, the course that you have settled now[16]
will bring in profit enough, for they make salt at Plymouth, and
have good store of boats, all which is means to bring in profit.
And I make no question now but that New Plymouth will quickly
return your money again. For the most part they are honest and
careful men. However, they have had many crosses; yet now
they will flourish, God blessing them, which God grant.

I do understand that Thomas Dawson, the surgeon,[17] hath
been very large on his tongue concerning myself, or that I
should be displaced by Mr. Bradford, and many other contume-

---

15. Letter of marque.   16. To seek profit in fishing.
17. Dawson, surgeon on the *Little James*, used language such that Altham "and

lious speeches, as also he informed you about the Frenchman. For all which, I pray, sir, if you see him, certify him that I will make him answer it in England; and although it cost £100, I will make him see the jail for it. And there he shall lie, if God bless me homeward. If it please God to deal otherwise with me, I pray God give him more grace, but I hope you do not believe him. But I would wish you rather suspect him, for he is the veriest villain that I ever knew, as hath been testified by his carriage both to Plymouth company, your own self and Company, and also to me. And truly, I fear that I shall justly lay that to his charge which if it be prosecuted will go near to hang him.

At this time I do expect news from our Governor, Mr. Bradford, and as I think, he will determine that we shall bring home Mr. Peirce[18] his cor-fish and train.[19] But I think it will fall out otherwise, for I have at this present received a letter from one of my acquaintance that is owner of a ship in this country, and he proffers me for to hire our ship and to take our men out and to put them into his own ship, which goeth for the Straits.[20] And so by this means I hope to get a good freight and to save wages and provisions for some of my own company. And this answer I have returned him: that I demand £140 for our ship, and to come for England presently; so that then we shall be defrayed of all charge and have our ship brought home for nothing. And indeed, we must be forced to come for England very soon, because we have no provisions nor have any means to get any. But of all these things I write in what I think, for I have (and ever will do) refer all these matters concerning your ship to the Governor and

---

others durst not go to sea with [him]; . . . such that we were constrained to dismiss him," and replace him with a man from the *Anne*. "A Letter of William Bradford and Isaac Allerton, 1623," *Am. Hist. Rev.*, VIII, 300.

18. Peirce and the *Charity* had gone to the fishing areas about the time of the wreck.

19. Oil extracted from fat-fleshed fish by heat or pressure. Fish other than cod had little market in Europe. In later centuries, the term, "train-oil," was given to whale oil.

20. Of Gibraltar.

his Assistants' directions; and if good suffer me, they shall be followed.

I pray, sir, let the 40s. I gave Mr. Mastige a bill for be paid at first sight, for he did me a great kindness in it; for otherwise I could not have got some bread which I did.

Thus my love being remembered to yourself and wife, with thanks for your token I received by Mr. Winslow, being three gallons of "hot water." Pray remember my love [to] Mr. Terrill Bacco, Mr. Stubs and his wife, your brother Robert, and Mr. John Sherley and his wife, to Mr. Brewer, Mr. Collier, Dr. Ran, Mr. Marshall, Mr. Thorrell, and to Mr. Pocop (my good friend), and especially to Robert Cushman, and all these the rest of my loving friends of the Company and out of the Company.[21]

And I pray, sir, if you please, let the Company see my letter. For look, what I have wrote to you in particular, so much would I have wrote to them in general, but time did wonderfully prevent me, in such manner that I am put to straits every way.

I pray remember me kindly to my two brothers and my sister, and the rest of my loving friends; and pray let them know I could not have time to write to them. Only I pray tell them I am well, and that I hope one day to see them again, but the time is uncertain. Yet I fear we shall come sooner than I desire, since our great expectation is so hindered by misfortune. But I do not doubt of the profit that may be raised the next year, for now you have laid as good a ground-plot as ever was—and better than before, for without this course of fishing, you cannot have your monies again.[22] Thus, praying to God daily for them and you and for all well-willers to this foreign plantation, I ever rest

yours and others', to my power,

EMMANUEL ALTHAM

21. Besides Robert Cushman, several of these men were probably Adventurers for New Plymouth—Thomas Brewer, William Collier, John Thornell, John Pocock.

22. English opinion, including Gov. Bradford's at this time, agreed that profit from New England would come by fishing. Many made money in this way, but the New Plymouth Company lost heavily by it.

I pray tell Mrs. Bridge I will save her husband's things for her, so much as we saved, it being almost all lost.

The haste of this messenger makes me forget divers things which I should have wrote to you of; but I hope all things will be for the best, seeing it can be no better. For be not discouraged at this bad news, but hope the next year for better, which I do promise, if you hold on the course begun.

Vale!

[Addressed:]   To the worthy and my most respected loving, kind friend, Mr. James Sherley, Treasurer for New Plymouth Adventurers, dwelling on London Bridge, at the Golden Horseshoe.

New England, the 28th of May [?], 1624.

Pray send these three letters to Mr. Nathaniel [Hawes] at the Three Cocks in Cheapside.

Emmanuel Altham to Sir Edward Altham

June 10, 1625.

Loving brother,

In regard of that near bond wherewith I am tied to you, I cannot but seek all opportunities to inform you how it fareth with me — and at this time the more, in regard I am so far separated from you in the remotest parts of the west. And at this time I desire to be the more large, knowing your expectations will be frustrated by me, by not coming into England, the cause of which hath happened accidentally. For considering with myself of the many troubles and crosses and losses, with much hindrance of my time, which happened unto me at my last being there, upon serious consideration with myself, I durst not put myself so soon upon the same so rawly again. For first, thinking with myself how ill I was dealt withal by Mr. Pemberton and his associates, for whose good I was up early and late, and whose ship I furnished with all manner of provisions, ready to take her voyage to sea;[1] yet, because there was a jar between him and the Adventurers I formerly served (whom I found always loving unto me and in whose service I being, I employed my body and mind for their good), he thought I had concealed some things from him, whereby he took himself prejudiced. Whereas, I, meaning

---

1. Mr. Pemberton, apparently a New Plymouth Adventurer and merchant, sent his ship under the sponsorship of the Dorchester Adventurers, the company founded under the inspiration of Rev. John White of Dorchester, which became the ancestor of the Massachusetts Bay Company. Pemberton probably was a close relative of another Adventurer, John Pemberton, a minister and enemy of the Leyden congregation Separatist element among the Plymouth settlers. John Pemberton received letters from John Lyford against the religious practices and government at Plymouth, and was a leader in the factional strife in the Company of Adventurers which led to its big split in 1625 after a debate over Lyford.

well, stood as neuter; which, if I had sticked to one side, I had done better—but if to him, not with a good conscience. For as heretofore I have related, he sought the overthrow of a whole colony of people, which since hath appeared more apparent. For at the arrival of Mr. Pemberton's ship and ours in this country, we both lighted upon one harbor,[2] where the New Plymouth Colony kept a stage for their fishing. Which stage they of Pemberton's ship, by order from him, seized upon by a wile; but in the interim were glad to compound, or else it had cost them the loss of their lives and ship. For the plantation sent twenty men in arms to regain it by land, and our ship[3] lay by theirs to fight with them if any onset were given. But they, loving to sleep in a whole skin, laid down their arms and abandoned the plantation's right; otherwise it had cost them some blood, if not their lives. Since which time, their agents here[4] do trouble this poor people, and have set factions among them, which I fear, in time, will be their overthrow, if God prevent it not in time. After which falling off with the one side in London, the other promised me more if I would serve them than I had demanded of the other; but they, as foolishly as the other side knavishly,[5] admitted so many of the Company for adventuring—and upon such terms which are too large to write, disheartened me from them likewise. For they would have had me to adventure £50 with them in ready money,

2. At Gloucester on Cape Ann, Mass.

3. *Hopewell*, William Peirce, master.

4. Lyford and Oldham, whose letters of complaint Bradford seized in 1624, continued their machinations against the Pilgrim church and government. Lyford had repented spectacularly after his first exposure, but went back to work, still believing he had more friends in the colony than dared speak up. He called down a list of complaints from the Pemberton party among the Adventurers, but only as they withdrew from the Company. Lyford and Oldham were exiled by the colonial government, Lyford leaving after a second exposure and Oldham after a period of near insanity, on the day when Altham arrived the second time.

5. The fools merely wanted to draw more capital to the sinking enterprise; the knaves had ulterior motives, probably inspired by Lyford's suggestion that every man sent to the settlement at Plymouth be given rights as an Adventurer (by juggling the accounts) in order to outvote the Bradford regime.

whereas others adventuring the like sum had a receipt for ten or twenty pounds more being upon old accounts. So in conclusion, I had cause to refuse both, or else to adventure my money I knew not how. After all which, it being left to my choice till the last, I made choice of this course: to expend some money in provisions for myself, and to live in the country here a little, that so I might not be censured for leaving off my voyage so fully intended. And although I went not in that nature I made account of, yet since my arrival here, which was upon the 4th of March, and seeing how things have been carried, I repent no whit, but rejoice in that I dealt with neither.

For my being here a while and marking the carriages of these fishing affairs, I doubt not but in time to manage them without the direction of others, which thing is the chiefest cause of my stay. For it is my resolution to adventure this ways again, but never to have any other but myself to be the chief manager of it, for a honest man had better deal with savages than with seamen, whose god is all manner of wickedness. And although the expense of my time will be much, yet as I shall not be any great gainer, so shall I be no great spender; yet I doubt not to be a safer, if God bless me in those courses that I will take. For I intend not to sit idle, but to use all means to help myself; and the next year, I hope to be settled in some certain course of plantation. It may be your acquaintance with Sir Samuel Argall[6] (if it be any) may do me some good, for I hear he intends to adventure for a plantation in this country the next year; in which business I doubt not but I could do him some good by reason of my acquaintance here with the natives. To which purpose I have writ to a merchant in London named Mr. Cross in Bartholomew Lane, who is of my acquaintance and the principal agent in that adven-

6. Argall, formerly associated with the Virginia Company, had become a leading member of the Council for New England. Other Council members took grants of land for themselves; Argall may have planned to, but he died on an English expedition to attack Cadiz in 1626.

ture. If you see it convenient, I pray speak to Sir Samuel, who I
know to be judicious and discreet and a lover to all plantations.

But for all this, I am not so wedded to my own desires as to re-
ject your good advice. For if you think it better for me to leave
this country than to tarry in it, showing your reasons, I will come
home to my own country the next year. But if I be not advised
by you to that purpose, my resolutions are settled here for some
longer time if I see any good to come of it. And in the mean time,
I pray excuse me to my friends who have expected me this year,
and according to your own discretion, frame them answer. However, I desire you, if Mr. Bland and William Watson enquire of
me, I pray pay them their monies for their adventure, if they do
in any sort suspect it or desire it; as also goodman Stracy and
Wells who, I know, long look for it, and from whose censures I
desire to be freed, although of right they should stand to the
hazard of profit and loss. But seeing it was adventured by my
means, I desire to repay them again, for I think that by reason of
Mr. Pemberton and his factions, a £10 share will never yield
twenty shillings. For he by his falsities made the Company in
England leave from supplying this people here, and now they
here will not join again with the Adventurers, but will live of
themselves.[7] I am right sorry that I have adventured so much
myself—much more that I persuaded you and some other friends
to adventure your monies in a business so strange to us all. But
it is too late; only I shall be more cautelous[8] while I live, and
look to my own better, for although that by these many mishaps
I have been a loser, yet I hope that my stock at home in your
hands will increase—if I be dealt honestly by, by them who had

7. Because of the debts contracted in their name by their agents and the London
merchants, the Plymouth settlers had to remain in the Company as reorganized by a
minority of the Adventurers headed by James Sherley. Between July and October,
1626, Isaac Allerton, as the colony's agent, arranged a deal to buy the interests of the
remaining Adventurers (including Altham) on an installment plan. Bradford, *Of
Plymouth Plantation*, 182–186; Bradford, "Letter Book," Mass. Hist. Soc., *Collections*,
1st ser., III, 48.
8. Wary, circumspect.

it when I came this way, which I hope you will take to your care. And for the more security of it, I desire you to take £400 of mine into your hands and to allow me an yearly annuity for it, such as in reason shall be thought fit by my brother Hawtry, my cousin Banks[9] and yourself. The other part of my means I will reserve to adventure when I see an opportunity, as being sufficient; which money, likewise, I refer to the care of you and my brother Hawtry to dispose of it as you think most for my good. But I pray you that those things I have sent for—which things are specified in a note here enclosed, let them all be bought for me, and let your man help Mr. Sherley to put them up for me in very good cask, for fear of wet. All which things are not for my private spending, but are to barter away to others to my most advantage. And to that end, let Mr. Sherley be furnished with monies, so that I may not fail of my expectations by the next shipping. I have also given Mr. Sherley order to receive £20 for me of one William Peirce, master of that ship I went over in the last year, being called the *Hopewell*. The said Peirce his bond I left with one Mr. Richard Tapper, grocer at Plymouth[10] by the town hall, who is my friend and did promise me to deliver it, it being enclosed in a letter directed to Mr. Sherley, if he were living, or to Mr. Nathaniel Hawes at the Three Cocks. Which bond, I hope, is come long before this time; but if it should not, I have given order to Mr. Sherley to send to him for it at the first receipt of my letter. And to Mr. Sherley hath Peirce promised me to deliver the money at his first coming into England, which will be about the 1st of September, 1625. In the mean time, pray solicit Mr. Sherley to do his best for me. Also to this Mr. Richard Tapper, grocer at Plymouth, and to one goodman Cheire, a throwster, who are both known to Mr. Sherley and are my friends. To them I have written to send me two hogsheads of white pease, two hogsheads of meal, four bushels of oatmeal, five hundred-

9. Hawtry's son-in-law, a lawyer.
10. Plymouth, England.

weight of biscuit, three or four she-goats, and four pair of leather buskins (to keep one free from the mosquitoes which are here infinite).

I pray, sir, do your best that these commodities be bought for me, which, if they come safe to me, I hope to make a good voyage of it. For all these things in the note are for the most part to trade with the Indians, which will make a good return, if God give me life and health—especially those knives and beads, of all which I have sent Mr. Sherley patterns of, with notes of their quantities, that I might have such as I have wrote for. I could have at this time sent home £20 worth of beaver, but I keep it by me for my more necessary occasions in trading. And if I can do nothing worthy my stay, I intend, if possibly, to see Virginia, and in my way homewards, to see Spain and France, that so I may be complete in travel, which will be worth my time.

Thus remembering my true love unto you with thankful acknowledgment of your continual care and love towards me, I desire you to remember my love to your wife, my sister, my aunt Wolley, Mr. Denn, and the rest of my friends whose names want of time makes me not mention. Especially, as I am most bound, pray forget me not, but remember my love and service to the right worshipful Sir John Leventhorpe and his Lady, and to all my brothers and sisters there.

Farewell!

So, committing you to the Lord['s] protection, I rest

your truly loving brother 'till death,

EMMANUEL ALTHAM.

Patuxet, this 10th of June, 1625.

This is my first letter.

I have sent you an Indian tobacco pipe, being the first and rarest that ever I saw. I desire you to keep it for my sake, it being a great king's pipe in this country. I have sent it by Mr. Winslow to deliver you with his own hands—who, if he doth meet you at London, pray gratify his pains with a pint of wine, for he is my loving friend, and one who cometh this way again about next November, by whom I do much desire to hear from you, and in whom I have put my trust to buy my commodities to trade with the Indians here. The pipe cannot be transformed to a better smell, for it doth stink exceedingly of Indian tobacco.

ISAACK DE RASIERES

Isaack de Rasieres (1595-1669 or later)

BORN in Holland, Isaack de Rasieres was sent to America by the Dutch West India Company in 1626 to be chief trading agent (*Opper Koopman*) for the Company and Secretary to the new Director-General of New Netherland, Peter Minuit. While duties in government and commerce impeded each other so much that he wanted to drop his Secretaryship, De Rasieres dealt with the Plymouth Colony in his dual capacity. After an encouraging exchange of letters, he went to visit Governor Bradford in October, 1627, to reach an agreement on trade between the two colonies. De Rasieres, a man who liked order and futilely tried to impose it on the fur trade under his control, saw in the Pilgrim colony much that he strove for in New Netherland.

Among the wares which De Rasieres took to start business was a large quantity of sewan (i.e., wampum or "wampumpeag"), the belts of beads made from parts of the shells of the quahog, whelk, or periwinkle, which served as a kind of money among Indians who traded with the Dutch. De Rasieres hoped to spread the use of this medium of exchange among the New England natives, and with the fifty fathoms purchased from him in 1627, the Pilgrims accomplished this aim in two years. But instead of taking a big portion of their profit to New Netherland to buy wampum, as De Rasieres had planned, the Plymouth traders found other sources of supply and quickly rose to first place in the fur trade in New England. Sewan was easy to get from coastal tribes; the supply could not be controlled by anyone, as the shell-fish which make the raw material are very numerous. So De Rasieres merely helped turn the trading ambitions of the Plymouth Colony from fish to fur, the means by which the province ultimately paid its debts to the last of the Adventurers.

Some time after his return to Fort Amsterdam, De Rasieres lost his position as a result of factional disputes among the employees of his Company, and returned to Holland. He married a niece of one of the directors of the West India Company in 1633 and went to Brazil with her four years later, in the Company's employ. Later information about him indicates only that he was still in Brazil in 1651, raised a family, and was thought to be in Barbados in 1669, after the Portuguese had ousted the Dutch from Brazil.

The text of De Rasieres' letter to Samuel Blommaert which follows is substantially that by William I. Hull (from the original in the National Archives at the Hague) in J. F. Jameson (ed.), *Narratives of New Netherland, 1609–1664* ("Original Narratives of Early American History"; 1909), 102–115. The fragment translated by J. A. C. Fagginger Auer in H. R. Shurtleff, *The Log Cabin Myth* (edited and with introduction by S. E. Morison; 1939), 106–107, has been incorporated in the Hull version, and the editor has changed the punctuation in spots and standardized proper nouns when possible. One sentence, partly omitted in other English versions, appears here thanks to translation by Prof. Rosalie Colie of Wesleyan University, who has kindly checked the rest of the English text against the Dutch. Notes by Jameson retained here have been marked, "J.F.J."

An earlier translation by J. Romeyn Brodhead, from a transcript of the Dutch original, appears in New York Hist. Soc., *Collections*, second series, II, 343–354. The Dutch text, edited by A. Eekhof, has been printed in *Nederlandsch Archief voor Kerkgeschiedenis*, new series, XV (1919), 249–280.

De Rasieres' letter bears no date. Statements in it indicate that it was written after his return to Holland probably in 1628 or 1629. Several pages are missing in the middle.

Isaack de Rasieres to Samuel Blommaert[1]

c. 1628.

Mr. Blommaert:

As I feel myself much bound to your service, and in return know not how otherwise to recompense you than by this slight memoir, (wherein I have in part comprised as much as was in my power concerning the situation of New Netherland and its neighbors, and should in many things have been able to treat of or write the same more in detail, and better than I have now done, but that my things and notes, which would have been of service to me herein, have been taken away from me), I will beg you to be pleased to receive this, on account of my bounden service, etc.

On the 27th of July, Anno 1626, by the help of God, I arrived with the ship, *The Arms of Amsterdam*, before the bay of the great Mauritius River,[2] sailing into it about a musket shot from Godyn's Point,[3] into Coenraet's Bay[4] (because there the greatest depth is, since from the east point there stretches out a sand bank on which there is only from 9 to 14 feet of water); then sailed on, northeast and north-northeast, to about half way from the low sand bank called Godyn's Point to the Hamels-Hoofden,[5] the mouth of the river, where we found at half ebb 16, 17, 18 feet water, and which is a sandy reef a musket shot broad, stretching

1. Blommaert was a merchant in Amsterdam and a director of the West India Company, 1622–29, 1636–42.
2. The official name of the Hudson River for several years (named after Maurice, Prince of Orange). "Mauritse" in the original.
3. Sandy Hook. [J. F. J.]
4. Sandy Hook Bay. [J. F. J.]
5. The Narrows, between Staten Island and Brooklyn.

for the most part northeast and southwest, quite across, and, according to my opinion, having been formed there by the stream, inasmuch as the flood runs into the bay from the sea, east-southeast; the depth at Godyn's Point is caused by the tide flowing out along there with such rapidity.

Between the Hamels-Hoofden the width is about a cannon's shot of 2,000 [yards]; the depth 10, 11, 12 fathoms. They are tolerably high points, and well wooded. The west point is an island, inhabited by from eighty to ninety savages, who support themselves by planting maize. The east point is a very large island,[6] full 24 leagues long, stretching east by south and east-southeast along the sea-coast, from the river to the east end of the Fisher's Hook.[7] In some places it is from three to four leagues broad, and it has several creeks and bays, where many savages dwell, who support themselves by planting maize and making sewan,[8] and who are called Siwanoys and Shinnecocks.[9] It is also full of oaks, elms, walnut and fir trees, also wild cedar and chestnut trees. The tribes are held in subjection by, and are tributary to, the Pyquans, hereafter named.[10] The land is in many places good, and fit for plowing and sowing. It has many fine valleys, where there is good grass. Their form of government is like that of their neighbors, which is described hereafter.

The Hamels-Hoofden being passed, there is about a league width in the river, and also on the west side there is an inlet, where another river runs up about twenty leagues,[11] to the north-northeast, emptying into the Mauritius River in the high-

6. Long Island.

7. Montauk Point.

8. Wampum.

9. The Siwanoys lived north of Long Island Sound, from the Bronx to Norwalk, Conn.; the Shinnecocks inhabited the east end of Long Island. "Souwenos," in the original, is a name applied promiscuously by early Dutch cartographers.

10. No doubt in the missing portion; the Pequots are apparently meant. [J. F. J.] The Pequots lived to the west of Narragansett Bay, in the eastern part of Connecticut.

11. Probably the Kill van Kull and the Passaic or Hackensack River was thought to connect with the Wallkill River and Rondout Creek.

lands, thus making the northwest land opposite to the Manhattas an island eighteen leagues long. It is inhabited by the old Manhattans; they are about two hundred to three hundred strong, women and men, under different chiefs, whom they call *Sackimas*. This island is more mountainous than the other land on the southeast side of the river, which opposite to the Manhattas is about a league and a half in breadth. At the side of the before-mentioned little river, which we call "Achter Col," there is a great deal of waste reedy land; the rest is full of trees, and in some places there is good soil, where the savages plant their maize, upon which they live, as well as by hunting. The other side of the same small river, according to conjecture, is about 20 to 23 leagues broad to the South River,[12] in the neighborhood of the Sancicans, in so far as I have been able to make it out from the mouths of the savages; but as they live in a state of constant enmity with those tribes, the paths across are but little used, wherefore I have not been able to learn the exact distance; so that when we wish to send letters overland, they (the natives) take their way across the bay, and have the letters carried forward by others, unless one amongst them may happen to be on friendly terms, and who might venture to go there.

The island of the Manhattas extends two leagues in length along the Mauritius River, from the point where the Fort "New Amsterdam" is building. It is about seven leagues in circumference, full of trees, and in the middle rocky to the extent of about two leagues in circuit. The north side has good land in two places, where two farmers, each with four horses, would have enough to do without much clearing at first. The grass is good in the forest and valleys, but when made into hay is not so nutritious for the cattle as here,[13] in consequence of its wild state, but it yearly improves by cultivation. On the east side there rises a large level field, of from 70 to 80 morgens of land,[14]

12. Delaware River.   13. In Holland. [J. F. J.]
14. A morgen is about two acres. [J. F. J.]

through which runs a very fine fresh stream; so that that land can be plowed without much clearing. It appears to be good. The six farms, four of which lie along the River Hellgate,[15] stretching to the south side of the island, have at least 60 morgens of land ready to be sown with winter seed, which at the most will have been plowed eight times. But as the greater part must have some manure, inasmuch as it is so exhausted by the wild herbage, I am afraid that all will not be sown; and the more so, as the managers of the farms are hired men. The two hindermost farms, Nos. 1 and 2, are the best; the other farms have also good land, but not so much, and more sandy; so that they are best suited for rye and buckwheat.

The small fort, New Amsterdam, commenced to be built, is situated on a point opposite to Noten Island;[16] [the channel between] is a gun-shot wide, and is full six or seven fathoms deep in the middle. This point might, with little trouble, be made a small island, by cutting a canal through Blommaert's Valley, so as to afford a haven winter and summer, for sloops and ships; and the whole of this little island ought, from its nature, to be made a superb fort, to be approached by land only on one side (since it is a triangle), thus protecting them both.[17] The river marks out, naturally, three angles; the most northern faces and commands, within the range of a cannon shot, the great Mauritius River and the land; the southernmost commands, on the water level, the channel between Noten Island and the fort, together with the Hellgate; the third point, opposite to Blommaert's Valley, commands the lowland. The middle part, which ought to be left as a market-place, is a hillock, higher than the

15. East River. The West India Company's six farms lay east of the present Bowery, and extended from a fresh-water swamp occupying the site of the present Roosevelt and James Streets northward to Eighteenth or Twentieth Street. [J. F. J.]

16. Governor's Island.

17. I.e., both Fort Amsterdam and the little island itself. Blommaert's Vly was a low, damp depression running northeast and southwest about on the line of the present Broad Street. [J. F. J.]

surrounding land, and should always serve as a battery, which might command the three points, if the streets should be arranged accordingly.

Up the river the east side is high, full of trees, and in some places there is a little good land, where formerly many people have dwelt, but who for the most part have died or have been driven away by the Wappenos.[18]

These tribes of savages all have a government. The men in general are rather tall, well proportioned in their limbs, and of an orange color, like the Brazilians; very inveterate against those whom they hate; cruel by nature, and so inclined to freedom that they cannot by any means be brought to work. They support themselves by hunting, and when the spring comes, by fishing. In April, May and June, they follow the course of these,[19] which they catch with a drag-net they themselves knit very neatly, of the wild hemp, from which the women and old men spin the thread. The kinds of fish which they principally take at this time are shad, but smaller than those in this country ordinarily are, though quite as fat, and very bony; the largest fish is a sort of white salmon, which is of very good flavor, and quite as large; it has white scales; the heads are so full of fat that in some there are two or three spoonfuls, so that there is good eating for one who is fond of picking heads. It seems that this fish makes them lascivious, for it is often observed that those who have caught any when they have gone fishing, have given them, on their return, to the women, who look for them anxiously. Our people give the same report; it is the same with them when they eat a great deal at one time, as can be shown by the shirts.

As an employment in winter they make sewan, which is an oblong bead that they make from cockle-shells, which they find

18. This name applies more properly to one of the Indian dialects spoken in the vicinity of Manhattan. J. G. Wilson (ed.), *The Memorial History of the City of New York* (1892), I, 49.

19. The fish. [J. F. J.]

on the sea-shore, and they consider it as valuable as we do money here, since one can buy with it everything they have. They string it, and wear it around the neck and hands; they also make bands of it, which the women wear on the forehead under the hair, and the men around the body; and they are as particular about the stringing and sorting as we can be here about pearls. They are very fond of a game they call *Senneca*, played with some round rushes, similar to the Spanish feather-grass, which they understand how to shuffle and deal as though they were playing with cards; and they win from each other all that they possess, even to the lappet with which they cover their private parts, and so they separate from each other quite naked. They are very much addicted to promiscuous intercourse. Their clothing is [so simple as to leave the body] almost naked. In the winter time they usually wear a dressed deer skin; some have a bear's skin about the body, some a coat of scales, some a covering made of turkey feathers which they understand how to knit together very oddly, with small strings. They also use a good deal of duffel cloth, which they buy from us, and which serves for their blanket by night, and their dress by day.

The women are fine looking, of middle stature, well proportioned, and with finely cut features, with long and black hair, and black eyes set off with fine eyebrows. They are of the same color as the men. They smear their bodies and hair with grease, which makes them smell very rankly. They are very much given to promiscuous intercourse.

They have a marriage custom amongst them, namely, when there is one who resolves to take a particular person for his wife, he collects a fathom or two of sewan, and comes to the nearest friends of the person whom he desires, to whom he declares his object in her presence, and if they are satisfied with him, he agrees with them how much sewan he shall give her for a bridal present. That being done, he then gives her all the Dutch beads he has, which they call *Machampe*, and also all sorts of trinkets.

If she be a young virgin, he must wait six weeks more before he can sleep with her, during which time she bewails or laments over her virginity, which they call *Collatismarrenitten*. All this time she sits with a blanket over her head, without wishing to look at anyone, or anyone being permitted to look at her. This period being elapsed, her bridegroom comes to her. He in the meantime has been supporting himself by hunting, and what he has taken he brings there with him; they then eat together with the friends, and sing and dance together, which they call *Kintikaen*. That being done, the wife must provide the food for herself and her husband, as far as breadstuffs are concerned, and [should they fall short] she must buy what is wanting with her sewan.

For this reason they are obliged to watch the season for sowing. At the end of March they begin to break up the earth with mattocks, which they buy from us for the skins of beavers or otters, or for sewan. They make heaps like molehills, each about two and a half feet from the others, which they sow or plant in April with maize, in each heap five or six grains; in the middle of May, when the maize is the height of a finger or more, they plant in each heap three or four Turkish beans, which then grow up with and against the maize, which serves for props, for the maize grows on stalks similar to the sugar-cane. It is a grain to which much labor must be given, with weeding and earthing-up, or it does not thrive; and to this the women must attend very closely. The men would not once look to it, for it would compromise their dignity too much, unless they are very old and cannot follow the chase. Those stalks which are low and bear no ears, they pluck up in August, and suck out the sap, which is as sweet as if it were sugar-cane. When they wish to make use of the grain for bread or porridge, which they call *Sappaen*, they first boil it and then beat it flat upon a stone; then they put it into a wooden mortar, which they know how to hollow out by fire, and then they have a stone pestle, which they know how to make them-

selves, with which they pound it small, and sift it through a
small basket, which they understand how to weave of the rushes
before mentioned. The finest meal they mix with lukewarm
water, and knead it into dough; then they make round flat little
cakes of it, of the thickness of an inch or a little more, which they
bury in hot ashes, and so bake into bread; and when these are
baked they have some clean fresh water by them in which they
wash them while hot, one after another; and it is good bread, but
heavy. The coarsest meal they boil into a porridge, as is before
mentioned, and it is good eating when there is butter over it,
but a food which is very soon digested. The grain being dried,
they put it into baskets woven of rushes or wild hemp, and bury
it in the earth, where they let it lie, and go with their husbands
and children in October to hunt deer, leaving at home with their
maize the old people who cannot follow. In December they return home, and the flesh which they have not been able to eat
while fresh, they smoke on the way, and bring it back with them.
They come home as fat as moles.

When a woman here addicts herself to fornication, and the
husband comes to know it, he thrashes her soundly, and if he
wishes to get rid of her, he summons the Sackima with her
friends, before whom he accuses her. And if she be found guilty,
the Sackima commands one to cut off her hair in order that she
may be held up before the world as a whore, which they call
poerochque; and then the husband takes from her everything that
she has, and drives her out of the house. If there be children,
they remain with her, for they are fond of them beyond measure.
They reckon consanguinity to the eighth degree, and revenge an
injury from generation to generation unless it be atoned for; and
even then there is mischief enough, for they are very revengeful.

And when a man is unfaithful, the wife accuses him before the
Sackima, which most frequently happens when the wife has a
preference for another man. The husband being found guilty,
the wife is permitted to draw off his right shoe and left stocking

(which they make of deer or elk skins, which they know how to prepare very broad and soft, and wear in the winter time); she then tears off the lappet that covers his private parts, gives him a kick behind, and so drives him out of the house; and then "Adam" scampers off.

It would seem that they are very libidinous — in this respect very unfaithful to each other; whence it results that they breed but few children, so that it is a wonder when a woman has three or four children, particularly by any one man whose name can be certainly known. They must not have intercourse with those of their own family within the third degree, or it would be considered an abominable thing.

Their political government is democratic. They have a chief Sackima whom they choose by election, who generally is he who is richest in sewan, though of less consideration in other respects. When any stranger comes, they bring him to the Sackima. On first meeting they do not speak; they smoke a pipe of tobacco. That being done, the Sackima asks, "Whence do you come?" The stranger then states that, and further what he has to say, before all who are present or choose to come. That being done, the Sackima announces his opinion to the people, and if they agree thereto, they give all together a sigh, *"He!"* and if they do not approve, they keep silence, and all come close to the Sackima, and each sets forth his opinion till they agree. That being done, they come all together again to the stranger, to whom the Sackima then announces what they have determined, with the reasons moving them thereto.

All travellers who stop over night come to the Sackima, if they have no acquaintances there, and are entertained by the expenditure of as much sewan as is allowed for that purpose. Therefore, the Sackimas generally have three or four wives, each of whom has to furnish her own seed-corn.

The Sackima has his fixed fine of sewan for fighting and causing blood to flow. When any are

[At least four pages of the letter are missing. In them, De Rasieres probably mentioned the occasion of his trip to Plymouth in September and October, 1627, and described the country along the way.]

Coming out of the river Nassau,[20] you sail east-and-by-north about fourteen leagues, along the coast, a half league from the shore, and you then come to "Frenchman's Point" at a small river where those of Patuxet have a house made of hewn oak planks, called Aptucxet,[21] where they keep two men, winter and summer, in order to maintain the trade and possession. Here also they have built a shallop, in order to go and look after the trade in sewan, in Sloup's Bay[22] and thereabouts, because they are afraid to pass Cape Malabar,[23] and in order to avoid the length of the way; which I have prevented for this year by selling them fifty fathoms of sewan, because the seeking after sewan by them is prejudicial to us, inasmuch as they would, by so doing, discover the trade in furs;[24] which if they were to find out, it would be a great trouble for us to maintain, for they already dare to threaten that if we will not leave off dealing with that people, they will be obliged to use other means. If they do that now, while they are yet ignorant how the case stands, what will they do when they do get a notion of it?

From Aptucxet the English can come in six hours, through

20. Blackstone River, Upper Narragansett Bay, and Sakonnet River.

21. The short cut across the base of Cape Cod, now taken by ships through the Cape Cod Canal, was used by the Plymouth settlers and the Indians, who went up Scusset creek on the north side and down the Manomet River on the southwest. The site of the trading post built on the Manomet, near Buzzard's Bay, has been excavated and the house restored. It is in the town of Bourne and can be reached as follows: "after crossing the Bourne Bridge over the Canal [heading toward Cape Cod], turn sharp right; next, bear left at a fork and follow Shore Road to signs indicating the Post; turn right under the railroad bridge and follow a dirt road through woods to the Post." Morison, *Story of the "Old Colony" of New Plymouth*, 131n.

22. Narragansett Bay.

23. Cape Cod, especially Monomoy Point.

24. In New Netherland and western New England, especially the Connecticut valley.

the woods, passing several little rivulets of fresh water, to New Plymouth,[25] the principal place in the district Patuxet, so called in their patent from His Majesty in England.

New Plymouth lies in a large bay to the north of Cape Cod, or Malabar, east and west from the said point[26] of the cape, which can be easily seen in clear weather. Directly before the commenced town lies a sand-bank,[27] about twenty paces broad, whereon the sea breaks violently with an easterly and east-northeasterly wind. On the north side there lies a small island[28] where one must run close along, in order to come before the town; then the ships run behind that bank and lie in a very good roadstead. The bay is very full of fish, of cod, so that the Governor before named has told me that when the people have a desire for fish they send out two or three persons in a sloop, whom they remunerate for their trouble, and who bring them in three or four hours' time as much fish as the whole community require for a whole day — and they muster about fifty families.

At the south side of the town there flows down a small river of fresh water, very rapid, but shallow, which takes its rise from several lakes in the land above, and there empties into the sea; where in April and the beginning of May, there come so many shad from the sea which want to ascend that river, that it is quite surprising. This river the English have shut in with planks, and in the middle with a little door, which slides up and down, and at the sides with trellice work, through which the water has its course, but which they can also close with slides.

At the mouth they have constructed it with planks, like an eel-pot, with wings, where in the middle is also a sliding door, and

25. De Rasieres, however, protested to Gov. Bradford that he had not walked "so far this three or four years, wherefore I fear my feet will fail me; so I am constrained to entreat you to afford me the easiest means" to get from the Aptucxet trading post to Plymouth. So the Governor sent a boat to pick him up at Scusset. Bradford, "Letter Book," Mass. Hist. Soc., *Collections*, 1st ser., III, 54.

26. On an east-and-west line from the outer tip of Cape Cod.

27. Plymouth Beach. [J. F. J.]

28. The Gurnet and Saquish Head.

with trellice work at the sides, so that between the two [dams]
there is a square pool, into which the fish aforesaid come swim-
ming in such shoals, in order to get up above, where they de-
posit their spawn, that at one tide there are 10,000 to 12,000
fish in it, which they shut off in the rear at the ebb, and close up
the trellices above, so that no more water comes in; then the
water runs out through the lower trellices, and they draw out
the fish with baskets, each according to the land he cultivates,
and carry them to it, depositing in each hill three or four fishes,
and in these they plant their maize, which grows as luxuriantly
therein as though it were the best manure in the world. And if
they do not lay this fish therein, the maize will not grow, so that
such is the nature of the soil.

New Plymouth lies on the slope of a hill stretching east towards the sea-coast, with a broad street about a cannon shot of
800 feet long, leading down the hill; with a [street] crossing in
the middle, northwards to the rivulet and southwards to the
land.[29] The houses are constructed of clapboards, with gardens
also enclosed behind and at the sides with clapboards, so that
their houses and courtyards are arranged in very good order,
with a stockade against sudden attack; and at the ends of the
streets there are three wooden gates. In the center, on the cross
street, stands the Governor's house, before which is a square
stockade upon which four patereros are mounted, so as to en-
filade the streets. Upon the hill they have a large square house,
with a flat roof, built of thick sawn planks stayed with oak beams,
upon the top of which they have six cannon, which shoot iron
balls of four and five pounds, and command the surrounding
country. The lower part they use for their church, where they
preach on Sundays and the usual holidays. They assemble by
beat of drum, each with his musket or firelock, in front of the
captain's door; they have their cloaks on, and place themselves

29. He reverses the actual bearings; and the street first mentioned was longer,
1,150 feet. [J. F. J.]

in order, three abreast, and are led by a sergeant without beat of drum. Behind comes the Governor, in a long robe; beside him on the right hand, comes the preacher with his cloak on, and on the left hand, the captain with his side-arms and cloak on, and with a small cane in his hand; and so they march in good order, and each sets his arms down near him. Thus they are constantly on their guard night and day.

Their government is after the English form. The Governor has his Council, which is chosen every year by the entire community, by election or prolongation of term. In inheritances they place all the children in one degree, only the eldest son has an acknowledgment[30] for his seniority of birth. They have made stringent laws and ordinances upon the subject of fornication and adultery, which laws they maintain and enforce very strictly indeed, even among the tribes which live amongst them. They speak very angrily when they hear from the savages that we live so barbarously in these respects, and without punishment. Their farms are not so good as ours, because they are more stony, and consequently not so suitable for the plow. They apportion their land according as each has means to contribute to the eighteen thousand guilders which they have promised to those who had sent them out;[31] whereby they have their freedom without rendering an account to anyone. (Only if the King should choose to send a governor-general, they would be obliged to acknowledge him as sovereign overlord.) The maize seed which they do not

30. A double share. [J. F. J.]
31. In 1626, Isaac Allerton on behalf of the Plymouth settlers, agreed to buy the interests of the remaining London Adventurers for £1800, which De Rasieres translated into guilders by a simple formula. In July 1627, though De Rasieres may not have been well informed of the event, a group of leading men in the Colony, led by Bradford, became "Undertakers" for six years to pay this debt (and about £600 in other debts owed by the Colony) by means of a monopoly on the external trade of the settlement, including all dealings with the Indians. According to the agreement, each colonist who was a Freeman of the Company (i.e., had agreed to the purchase in 1626 and acquired rights to a share in the division of lands) made an annual payment to the Undertakers of three bushels of corn or six pounds of tobacco as they might specify. Bradford, *Of Plymouth Plantation*, 184–188, 194–196.

require for their own use is delivered over to the Governor, at three guilders the bushel, who in his turn sends it in sloops to the north for the trade in skins among the savages; they reckon one bushel of maize against one pound of beaver's skins; the profits are divided according to what each has contributed, and they are credited for the amount in the account of what each has to contribute yearly towards the reduction of his obligation. Then with the remainder they purchase what next they require, and which the Governor takes care to provide every year. They have better sustenance than ourselves, because they have the fish so abundant before their doors. There are also many birds, such as geese, herons and cranes, and other small-legged birds, which are in great abundance there in the winter.

The tribes in their neighborhood have all the same customs as already above described, only they are better conducted than ours, because the English give them the example of better ordinances and a better life; and who also, to a certain degree, give them laws, in consequence of the respect they from the very first have established amongst them.

The savages utilize their youth in labor better than the savages round about us: the young girls in sowing maize, the young men in hunting. They teach them to endure privation in the field in a singular way, to wit:

When there is a youth who begins to approach manhood, he is taken by his father, uncle, or nearest friend, and is conducted blindfolded into a wilderness, in order that he may not know the way, and is left there by night or otherwise, with a bow and arrows, and a hatchet and a knife. He must support himself there a whole winter with what the scanty earth furnishes at this season, and by hunting. Towards the spring they come again, and fetch him out of it, take him home and feed him up again until May. He must then go out again every morning with the person who is ordered to take him in hand. He must go into the forest to seek wild herbs and roots, which they know to be the most poisonous and bitter; these they bruise in water and press the juice out of them, which he must drink, and immediately have ready such herbs as will preserve him from death or vomiting. And if he cannot retain it, he must repeat the dose until he can support it, and until his constitution becomes accustomed to it so that he can retain it.

Then he comes home, and is brought by the men and women, all singing and dancing, before the Sackima; and if he has been able to stand it all well, and if he is fat and sleek, a wife is given to him.

In that district there are no lions or bears, but there are the same kinds of other game, such as deers, hinds, beavers, otters, foxes, lynxes, seals and fish, as in our district of country. The savages say that far in the interior there are certain beasts of the size of oxen, having but one horn, which are very fierce. The English have used great diligence in order to see them, but cannot succeed therein, although they have seen the flesh and hides of them which were brought to them by the savages. There are also very large elks there, which the English have indeed seen.

The lion skins which we sometimes see our savages wear are not large, so that the animal itself must be small; they are of a mouse-gray color, short in the hair and long in the claws.

The bears are some of them large and some small; but the largest are not so large as the middle-sized ones which come from Greenland. Their fur is long and black and their claws large. The savages esteem the flesh and grease as a great dainty.

Of the birds, there is a kind like starlings, which we call "maize thieves," because they do so much damage to the maize. They fly in large flocks, so that they flatten the corn in any place where they alight, just as if cattle had lain there. Sometimes we take them by surprise and fire amongst them with hail-shot, immediately that we have made them rise, so that sixty, seventy, and eighty fall all at once, which is very pleasant to see.

There are also very large turkeys living wild; they have very long legs, and can run extraordinarily fast, so that we generally take savages with us when we go to hunt them; for even when one has deprived them of the power of flying, they yet run so fast that we cannot catch them unless their legs are hit also.

In the autumn and in the spring there come a great many geese, which are very good, and easy to shoot, inasmuch as they congregate together in such large flocks. There are two kinds of partridges; the one sort are quite as small as quails and the other like the ordinary kind here. There are also hares, but few in number, and not larger than a middle-sized rabbit; and they principally frequent where the land is rocky.

This, sir, is what I have been able to communicate to you from memory, respecting New Netherland and its neighborhood, in discharge of my bounden duty. I beg that the same may so be favorably received by you, and I beg to recommend myself for such further service as you may be pleased to command me in, wherever you may find me.

In everything your faithful servant,

ISAACK DE RASIERES.

Bibliographical Note

The standard sources of information on early Plymouth are quickly named: William Bradford, *Of Plymouth Plantation* (1952, or other edition); the items in Alexander Young (ed.), *Chronicles of the Pilgrim Fathers* (1844), most of which were printed for "Everyman's Library" under the same title, 1910; and G. F. Willison, *The Pilgrim Reader* (1953). Other books which proved useful in the preparation of this one have been cited in footnotes. In addition to these, several ought to receive notice.

On John Pory there are articles in *Dictionary of National Biography* (by Charlotte Fell-Smith) and *Dictionary of American Biography* (by A. C. Gordon, Jr.). See also Leo Africanus, *The History and Description of Africa*, translated by John Pory, ed. and intro. by Robert Brown (1896); W. F. Craven, *Dissolution of the Virginia Company* (1932) and *The Southern Colonies in the Seventeenth Century* (1949); S. M. Kingsbury (ed.), *Records of the Virginia Company of London* (1933, 1935), III, IV; Mass. Hist. Soc., *Collections*, fourth series, IX, 8–47; J. H. R. Yardley, *Before the Mayflower* (1931).

Emmanuel Altham's name until now has been virtually missing from the Pilgrim literature. The late Dr. Otto Fisher, of Detroit, had a file containing such information as exists on Altham and his family, compiled by Victor C. Sanborn and Oliver R. Barrett with the aid of correspondents in England. Dr. Fisher kindly let the editor of this volume use the file.

The life of Isaack de Rasieres is covered and illuminated by J. F. Jameson, "Introduction" to "Letter of Isaack de Rasieres to Samuel Blommaert, 1628 (?)," *Narratives of New Netherland, 1609–1664* ("Original Narratives of Early American History";

1909), 98–99; and "Letter from Isaack de Rasière to the Amsterdam Chamber of the West India Company, September 23, 1626," in A. J. F. van Laer (translator and editor), *Documents Relating to New Netherland, 1624–1626, in the Henry E. Huntington Library* (1924), 171–251, 260–276. See also A. C. Flick (editor), *History of the State of New York* (1933), I, II.

About New England in general and the fishing business, see also C. F. Adams, *Three Episodes in Massachusetts History* (1894), I; C. K. Bolton, *The Real Founders of New England* (1929); I. S. Proper, *Monhegan the Cradle of New England* (1930); Frances Rose-Troup, *John White the Patriarch of Dorchester* (1930) and *The Massachusetts Bay Company and its Predecessors* (1930); C. K. Shipton, *Roger Conant of Massachusetts* (1945); and William Vaughan, *The Golden Fleece* (London, 1626), Part III.

Index

CPSIA information can be obtained at www.ICGtesting.com
Printed in the USA
BVOW04s2230050914

365686BV00001B/8/A